AF174119

Dear Student,

As a college counselor I saw many students who were frustrated and discouraged with their attempts to make a decision about a major or career. I believe part of the problem may be our rather naïve perception that we can do anything if it pays enough money and has enough status.

We probably are capable of doing almost anything we set our minds to. However, knowledge of our personality preferences will help us understand why we are not motivated to do just anything.

By nature we are motivated toward certain pursuits and not others. Being aware of our personality preferences brings focus in life and helps us choose careers that will enhance our inherent gifts and talents. Without this knowledge, we remain scattered and unfocused.

This workbook will guide you through this new concept in understanding who you are and focusing on your natural strengths. You will be taken on a journey of self-discovery—one that will lead you in making meaningful decisions in school, work and life.

I know you will find this experience rewarding if you commit to completing this workbook. You may also want to read the companion book **Follow Your Inner Heroes™ To The Work You Love.** In any event, I wish you fun and success as you discover your true self and move toward the work you'll love!

Sincerely,

Carolyn Kalil
Counselor

This latest work by Carolyn Kalil has a great new look, and has been fully revised to include updated career information, as well as new proven approaches for career selection developed by Ms. Kalil in the classroom over the last 25 years.

As Ms. Kalil wrote in her introductory "Dear Student" letter, **The Workbook** is a companion to her 1998 book, **Follow Your Inner Heroes™ To The Work You Love,** which is now in its 15th printing. Although each book stands on its own, together they offer a complete and fun course of study for discovering your life's work.

Now, get ready to enjoy discovering your natural strengths and skills, and uncovering your pathway to the work you love.

ISBN 978-0-9858530-7-5
Former ISBN 978-0-9858530-2-0
Former ISBN 978-1-893320-20-8

Fifth Edition
Tenth Printing August 2012
Eleventh Prining April 2013

Printed in the United States of America.

Follow Your Inner Heroes™ To The Work You Love

The Workbook

Create Success in College, Work and Life

Carolyn Kalil, M.A.

DreamMaker Publishing, Inc.
PO Box 2804
Malibu, CA 90265
www.innerheroes.com
Support@innerheroes.com

About the Author

Carolyn Kalil is author of the best selling book Follow Your Inner Heroes™ To The Work You Love. She is also recognized internationally as a speaker, life purpose counselor, and coach. Carolyn believes there is something unique within each of us and her message always begins with self understanding.

Carolyn is the past president of the National Employment Counseling Association, a division of the American Counseling Association (ACA).

She earned her BA degree in Elementary Teaching in 1970 and her M.A. in Counseling in 1973 from Ohio State University. She taught elementary school for 2 years in South Central Los Angeles before beginning her 32 year counseling career at UCLA and El Camino Community College.

Carolyn Kalil is a retired counselor from El Camino Community College in Southern California and author of the books Follow Your Inner Heroes™ To The Work You Love, and True Success.

ckalil@innerheroes.com
www.innerheroes.com

Table of Contents

Preface

Why I wrote this workbook

A majority of students I have counseled since 1973 have expressed a fear of investing time, energy, and money toward making the wrong career choice. Time and again, they demonstrated strong resistance to spending several years in college preparing for a career they did not feel highly motivated to pursue. And their counseling sessions typically ended up focusing on a career decision, regardless of the initial reason for the appointment.

On many occasions, these students have come to me with personal problems related to study habits, but the nature of their problem was generally the same: They had lost interest in school because of indecision as to their futures. These students lacked direction and found it difficult to focus on school and studies. Some were experiencing conflicts with parents, family, and spouses as a result of dropping grades and lack of motivation.

A knowledge of personality preferences through temperament theory has helped me tremendously in understanding the natural gifts, talents, and values of students and directing them toward careers they will find truly satisfying. Its clear, definitive methods for finding success and enhancing self-esteem are invaluable. And once you begin this workbook, I am confident you will want to integrate the program into your academic, personal, and career endeavors. It will be a journey well worth your time and effort and will impact all segments of your life.

There is only one success -- to be able to spend your life in your own way.
-Christopher Morley

INTRODUCTION

Chapter 1
Introduction

Theoretical Base

This workbook is based on the belief that we have intrinsic characteristics which drive our human behavior and through which we strive to experience self-esteem. As a result, we are imprinted with specific ways of thinking, understanding, valuing, and conceptualizing.

Our behavior, therefore, manifests certain attitudes, preferences, wants, aims, needs, motives, and desires that make us feel good about ourselves. These predispositions drive our actions and habits, making our behavior predictable in all contexts of our lives.

This theory of individual differences is not new and traces to Hippocrates, who 25 centuries ago identified four different types of human beings in his 1921 release of Psychological Type.

Soon after, Isabel Myers Briggs developed the now famous Myers Briggs Type Indicator which states that human behavior is quite orderly and can be characterized by 16 different personality types.

Dr. David Keirsey has been refining the work of Myers Briggs for the past 35 years. His book, Please Understand Me, reflects the basis of the "Inner Heroes" philosophy.

I use the Inner Heroes as a metaphor for understanding human characteristics and how intrinsic behavior must be differentially rewarded. The Inner Heroes are the Thinker, Planner, Helper and the Doer — that will be used herein to represent each temperament type.

Inner Heroes™ as compared to Keirsey's temperament and True Colors:

Heroes		Keirsey	True Colors
Helper	=	NF	Blue
Planner	=	SJ	Gold
Thinker	=	NT	Green
Doer	=	SP	Orange

The Meaning of the Inner Heroes

What is a hero? Today we use this term to refer to someone we greatly admire and respect. It may be a person of outstanding accomplishments or someone who displays great courage when faced with danger and adversity. Yet, a hero doesn't have to be famous to gain this status. It may be an ordinary person in your life who is a role model for how you want to live your life.
The Inner Heroes I refer to in this workbook represent the unique characteristics within each one of us. They are the qualities that cannot be seen because they are hidden inside of us but they are expressed through our personality traits. This book makes these hero qualities visible so that you can use them to discover the work you love. As Mariah Carey sang,
"Look inside you and be strong
And you finally see the truth
That a hero lies in you."

The four primary Heroes are Thinker, Planner, Doer, and Helper. Each express different dominant characteristics. You express all of these traits but the dominant Hero within you represents the qualities you express most often. You will understand what this means when you take the quiz in the next chapter.

Helper:
Of all the people in the world, Helpers are the most loving, nurturing and supportive. They do not have to work at it, it is simply their amazing nature — who they are. Everyone has special gifts and talents and Helpers possess extraordinary people skills.

Helpers do not strive for power or control. Instead, they have an uncompromising dedication to helping others feel good about themselves. Helping is what they most enjoy, even if they are not paid to do it. To raise a person's self-esteem or help someone reach a goal gives a Helper more personal satisfaction than money could ever buy. Money is seen as a tool to achieve ideals rather than a way to gain power or status, or impress other people.

Thinker
They are the exceptionally deep and brilliant thinkers of the world. When describing Thinkers, others typically use words like intelligent, clever, wise, and witty. They are remembered as the ones who got the better

grades in school, and they often rise to leadership roles.

To Thinkers, knowledge is power, and their insatiable thirst for knowledge is what drives them. This behavior can be observed in scientists, who typically are Thinkers. The university professor who is paid to acquire knowledge continually through research is also an example of this personality. Research and development is an ideal career for some Thinkers.

Planner

If you want something done, give it to a Planner. They are dependable and reliable and can be counted on to do what they say and be where they are supposed to be in a timely manner. If they say they will meet you at eight o'clock, they mean eight o'clock sharp — not five after eight. Punctuality is important to them. In fact, arriving early to make sure they are not late is not unusual.

Planning everything is important. To Planners, not to plan is foolish. They don't like to be caught by surprise, and planning provides the predictability that they need. My Planner friends always know in advance what they are doing on a daily basis. I've learned never to ask them to do anything at the last minute.

Doer

Without the magnificent, upbeat and light-hearted personality of the Doer, the rest of us would probably forget how to have fun. The most likely place to find a Doer is anywhere people are laughing and having a good time. Many get paid to entertain us. Typically they are the ones at the center of attention. Most Doers are extroverted characters with little modesty, although some are laid back and quiet.

Doers' attitude is "live for today, for tomorrow is not promised." Consequently, it is difficult for them to save, store or prepare. What if tomorrow never comes? They live life in the present — what is happening right now is most important. They don't take life as seriously as other types, because they know life is supposed to be fun.

How does this Hero personality theory impact career planning? If differences make behavior predictable in all contexts, this would also hold true in career decision-making. The subsequent chapters will assist each of the Hero groups in making career decisions that are consistent with who they are.

A Career Versus A Job

A career is much more than a job. A job is a series of tasks performed for pay, usually without much preparation or concern for personal growth or enjoyment.

A career, on the other hand, encompasses all of the job characteristics, and more. One needs to prepare for a career by obtaining required training or education. A career accounts for who a person is, making personality, interests, values, and skills integral parts of a career decision. These considerations allow a career-minded person to continue to grow and to develop, thereby encouraging individual expression and enhanced satisfaction in one's work.

Why Plan A Career?

Generally speaking, most working Americans do not enjoy the work they do. This is because they have chosen a job rather than plan a career that expresses who they are. Since most of us will work 40 hours each week the majority of our lives, the quality of our lives depends greatly on what we do during those precious hours.

The most important component of career planning involves self-understanding. The following chapters will help you understand yourself more thoroughly than ever before. Then you will gather occupational information to assist you in making decisions and setting goals toward a career that can become your life's work.

Exercise 1

Pre-test

How well do you know your strengths? You began this workbook with certain beliefs about the things that you do well. List below all the things you are good at doing. You will learn more later in this workbook about your real strengths.

My strengths are:

1.

2.

3.

4.

5.

6.

7.

8.

9.

10.

Exercise 2

Criteria for selecting a career

Extrinsic factors (those that satisfy external needs)	Intrinsic factors (those that satisfy deeper personal needs)
1.	1.
2.	2.
3.	3.
4.	4.
5.	5.

"For a career to be satisfying and have a sense of purpose, extrinsic factors need to be secondary to intrinsic factors."

1-minute essay
Discuss why you agree or disagree with the above statement

_____

_____

_____

_____

_____

_____

_____

Exercise 3

Outstanding attributes

List your outstanding attributes.

My name:

My outstanding attributes: _____

_____

_____

_____

_____

_____

Write the name of someone you know and list their outstanding attributes.

Name:

Attributes:_____

_____

_____

_____

_____

_____

Write a one-minute essay explaining which list is longer. Why?

_____

_____

_____

_____

_____

_____

Exercise 4

What does success mean to you?

_____

_____

_____

_____

_____

_____

_____

Success is a public affair, failure is a private funeral.
--Rasalind Russel

Nothing succeeds like success.
– Alexander Dumas

_____

_____

_____

_____

_____

Exercise 5

Spending your money

Congratulations! You have just won the $10 million lottery. Now what will you do with your time? Describe the kind of work you would do to make a contribution to society.

_____

_____

_____

_____

_____

_____

_____

_____

Which of the things described above could you begin doing now?

_____

_____

_____

_____

_____

_____

_____

Exercise 6

Where are you now?

What are some of the college majors you have considered?

_____

_____

_____

How do you presently feel about each one?

_____

_____

_____

What subjects do you enjoy most?

_____

_____

_____

Why did you make the decision to go to college?

_____

_____

_____

_____

How committed are you to staying in school?

_____

_____

_____

_____

Who is supporting you in reaching your goals?

_____

_____

_____

Chapter 1

Short Journal (5 minutes or less)

Do you feel your life is moving in the direction you want it to go? Why or Why not?

_____

_____

_____

_____

_____

_____

_____

_____

_____

_____

_____

_____

_____

Knowing others is wisdom. Knowing the self is enlightenment.
– Lao-tzu

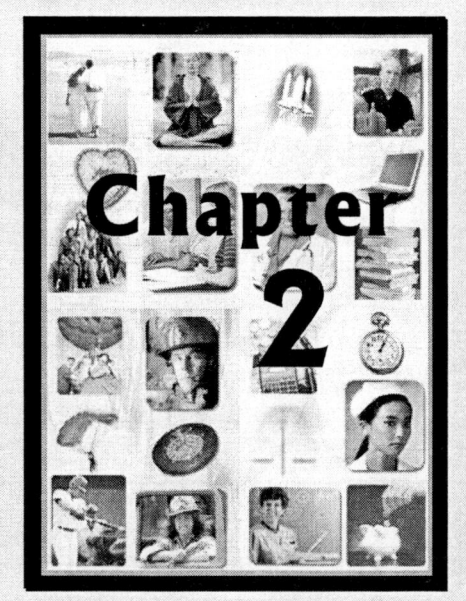

Chapter 2

WHO AM I?

Chapter 2

Who am I?

I cannot stress enough the value in understanding yourself as the first step in career decision-making. This knowledge allows you to direct your energies, focus your attention, and find a career that is compatible and satisfying.

This chapter, as well as the following three, will focus on self-understanding. Without such an understanding, career planning would be like reading want ads without knowing which offering best suits you. Instead, you must determine those things you are naturally inspired to do—what you spend time doing because you enjoy it, not because you are being paid to perform or produce.

I believe we all have natural gifts and talents which can lead us in the direction of an enjoyable and fulfilling career. But all too often, someone close to us convinces us we cannot do something, or we are unable to overcome fears about pursuing a certain goal. Whatever the reason, we must ask ourselves how much it is worth to go for what we really want.

For an understanding of what it is like to be engaged in dissatisfying work, simply observe employees at some of the local businesses you frequent. Do they exhibit a lack of enthusiasm? Is their service courteous? You can avoid such pitfalls by learning to make career decisions based on who you are, what you enjoy doing, and your natural strengths.

However, some people base their career decisions solely on income. While income is a natural consideration when planning a career, I believe that those persons creative enough to base a career on what they enjoy doing will also use that creativity to ensure sufficient financial reward. An example is the young man who told me he enjoyed wrecking his toys as a young boy and now is very successful in the demolition business.

On the next page, you can begin your journey of self-understanding—a journey that will lead you in the direction of an exciting career.

It is not easy to find happiness in ourselves, and it is not possible to find it elsewhere
– Agnes Repplier

Because families have a major impact on shaping our lives, writing about our past can help us understand who we are as a result of those experiences. Complete the following exercises and begin to better understand yourself!

Exercise 1

Family experiences

Describe your home experience as a child. Include such things as how many children in your family, birth order, your general emotional state (happy, sad, etc.), your relationship with each parent.

_____

_____

_____

_____

_____

_____

_____

_____

_____

_____

Give a little love to a child, and you get a great deal back.
– John Ruskin

_____

_____

_____

_____

_____

_____

What messages did you receive about who you are from your parents and other family members?

_____

_____

_____

_____

_____

_____

_____

_____

_____

Parents must get across the idea that "I love you always, but sometimes I do not love your behavior."
– Amy Vanderbilt

_____

_____

_____

_____

_____

_____

_____

_____

Exercise 2

Beliefs

What is the relationship between what you learned about yourself from your family members and your own beliefs about yourself today?

_____

_____

_____

_____

_____

_____

Man is what he believes
– Anton Chekhov

Which beliefs do not serve you and need to be changed? (In a later chapter you will learn how to change negative thought patterns into positive ones.)

Beliefs

1.

2.

3.

4.

5.

6.

7.

8.

9.

10.

Chapter 2

Short Journal (5 minutes or less)

Write about something you have learned about yourself.

_____

_____

_____

_____

_____

_____

_____

_____

_____

_____

_____

_____

_____

_____

_____

_____

_____

_____

_____

**And in the end
The love you take
Is equal to the love you
make.**
– John Lennon &
Paul McCartney

The cards you hold in the game of live means very little - - it's the way you play that counts.

MY INNER HEROES

Chapter 3

Identifying Your Personality Style

My Personality Inner Heroes

The following exercise will introduce you to your Heroes and assist you on a journey of knowing who you are. This knowledge will allow you to be an active participant in life rather than a passenger or a bystander.

Identifying Your Personality Heroes

Step 1

Take out your four Hero cards in the front jacket. Look at the pictures on the front and the words on the back and arrange the cards in the order from the most like you to the least like you.

Step 2

Go to the quiz on the next page. On each ROW, put a 4, 3, 2 or 1 in each box with 4 being the most like you and 1 being the least like you. Do this for each row. Then just add up the numbers in each column and enter this in the TOTAL row at the end of the quiz. The column with the highest score is your first Hero, the one with the lowest score is your last Hero. If there is a tie, use the order of the card sort to break the tie.

Arranging Your Personality Heroes

Now that you have sorted your Hero Cards and discovered and read about yourself and taken the quiz, have you identified your personality profile? There is also an online quiz available at both www.innerheroes.com and www.carolynkalil.com

Write your profile below.

To love and be loved

My primary Hero: _____
                        (The Hero most like you)

My Secondary Hero   _____
                        (The Hero next most like you)

And   _____
                             (The Hero of your third choice)

With   _____
                             (A weaker Hero of your last choice)

You now know your strongest Hero, the one you most identify with. The characteristics9 of your other Heroes vary in importance and the characteristics of your weakest Hero are least expressed in your behavior.

Using Your Cards with Others

Keep your Hero Cards to use with others. Your friends will have a natural interest in playing them with you. And once you understand their Personality profile, you can utilize the guide to improve communication, as well as your personal, academic, and professional success.

Exercise 1

Begin your Hero's assessment is on the next page.

I'm beautiful in my way 'Cause God makes no mistakes I'm on the right track, baby I was born this way

– LADY GAGA –
BORN THIS WAY
LYRICS

	Column A	Column B	Column C	Column D
1. Careers that are more appealing to me	☐ Allow me to express my ideas	☐ Allow me to build self-esteem in others	☐ Make me feel responsible and productive	☐ Contain a lot of activity and variety
2. I prefer to read a book about	☐ Famous great thinkers	☐ Love and romance	☐ A practical method to improve my life	☐ An exciting adventure
3. In my leisure time I	☐ Read something interesting or watch Discovery Channel	☐ Enjoy spending time with friends	☐ Do something productive	☐ Find something fun to do
4. When I make decisions	☐ I use logic and facts	☐ I rely on my feelings	☐ I trust what has proven to work in the past	☐ I go with what seems right at the time
5. In order to solve a problem I need to	☐ Analyze the situation & think of all possible solutions	☐ Know how the solution will effect people	☐ Make sure the solution is practical enough to work	☐ Give something a try and see how it works
6. The kind of person I enjoy spending time with	☐ Is intelligent	☐ Is sensitive to other people's feelings	☐ Is sensible and down to earth	☐ Likes to have a good time
7. The kind of subjects that interest me are related to	☐ Science and/or math	☐ Language and/or behavioral sciences	☐ History and politics	☐ Creative arts such as music, art and theatre
8. I learn best from instructors who	☐ Provide stimulating lectures that include theories	☐ Encourage interaction and group projects	☐ Explain information in a step-by-step manner	☐ Present information in a fun and entertaining way
9. In most things I do I am	☐ An independent thinker	☐ Considerate of other people's feelings	☐ Cautious	☐ Spontaneous
10. Others would describe me as	☐ Knowledgeable	☐ Compassionate	☐ Conservative	☐ Active

	THINKER	HELPER	PLANNER	DOER
11. The best movies	☐ Challenge how I think	☐ Appeal to my emotions	☐ Express moral values	☐ Have lots of action and excitement
12. What others would most likely find in my office	☐ Credentials, certificates, degrees	☐ Pictures of angels, people and/or animals	☐ A neatly organized space	☐ A variety of things on the walls and all over the desk
13. Which appeals to me more	☐ Being competent	☐ Being kind	☐ Being responsible	☐ Being busy
14. Which describes me best	☐ I am curious	☐ I am harmonious	☐ I am organized	☐ I am courageous
15. Complete this sentence - Most of the time I am	☐ Rational	☐ Sensitive	☐ Serious	☐ Spontaneous
16. I prefer to be thought of by others	☐ As smart	☐ As loving	☐ As dependable	☐ As fun
17. I have a tendency to be	☐ Logical	☐ Emotional	☐ Methodical	☐ Impulsive
18. I am more fulfilled with work that	☐ Is mentally challenging	☐ Helps others improve their personal lives	☐ Rewards me for my accomplishments	☐ Has some hands-on involvement
19. I prefer to work with others who are	☐ Intelligent	☐ Good team players	☐ Hard workers	☐ Fun to be with
20. Rules need to	☐ Make logical sense	☐ Have some room for heart	☐ Be followed by everyone	☐ Have some flexibility
TOTALS	THINKER	HELPER	PLANNER	DOER

Knowledge is Power.

Exercise 2

Autograph signing

Sign your name in your preferred hand (the hand you usually write with).

Now sign your name in your non-preferred hand (the other hand).

What was your experience when you wrote with your:

preferred hand?:

non-preferred hand?:

I'm starting with the man in the mirror
I'm asking him to change his ways
And no message could have been any clearer
If you wanna make the world a better place
Take a look at yourself and then make a change
Man In The Mirror
Songwriters:
Ballard, Glen;
Garrett, Siedah

Just as you have a preference for one hand, you also have preferences for certain personality characteristics.

Exercise 3

My Hero preferences

Why I think _____ is my first Hero

_____

_____

_____

_____

_____

_____

Why I think _____ is my second Hero

_____

_____

_____

_____

_____

_____

Where's the action?

Why I think _____ is my third Hero

_____

_____

_____

_____

_____

_____

_____

_____

Why I think _____ is my fourth Hero

_____

_____

_____

_____

_____

_____

Plan it!

Are you more extroverted or introverted?

Extroverts:
- usually relate more to their outer world of people and things than to their inner world of ideas.
- are often good at greeting people
- usually communicate well
- often don't mind being interrupted by answering the telephone.
- usually like having people around them

Introverts:
- usually relate more easily to their inner world of ideas than to their outer world of people and things.
- prefer quiet for concentration
- sometimes have problems communicating
- usually dislike telephone interruptions
- like to work alone

Life is what happens to you
While you're busy making other plans
– John Lennon

Exercise 4

Extroverted or introverted?

Discuss whether you are introverted, extroverted, or somewhere in between.

I consider myself to be more _____ than _____ because

_____

_____

_____

_____

_____

Or

I believe I am somewhere in between the two extremes because

_____

_____

_____

_____

Your Role Versus Your Identity

People often confuse the roles—student, sister, brother, friend , employee—they play in life with their identity. Your identity is who you are and your Inner Heroes help you understand your true self. It determines how you will naturally behave in a particular role, but the role does not change who you are. The more you can be your true self in these roles, the happier you will be.

Exercise 5

The Roles I play

Describe three roles you play. Are you expressing your true self in each one?

Role #1_____

Description

_____

_____

I do or do not feel like I express my true self in this role because

_____

_____

Role #2_____

Description

_____

_____

I do or do not feel like I express my true self in this role because

_____

_____

I hope you still feel small when you stand beside the ocean Whenever one door closes I hope one more opens Promise me that you'll give faith a fighting chance And when you get the choice to sit it out or dance

I hope you dance
Lee Ann Womack
Writers: TIA SILLERS, MARK D. SANDERS

Role #3_____

Description

_____

_____

I do or do not feel like I express my true self in this role because

_____

_____

_____

Exercise 6

A successful role

Imagine and describe yourself in a successful role that you would like to play.

_____

_____

_____

_____

_____

_____

What personality characteristics do you express in this role?

_____

_____

_____

_____

_____

_____

What would have to change in your life for you to play this ideal role?

_____

_____

_____

_____

_____

_____

Living is easy with eyes closed Misunderstanding all you see

Strawberry Fields
John Lennon,
Paul McCartney

Chapter 3

Short Journal (5 minutes or less)

What I have learned about myself in this chapter is:

_____

_____

_____

_____

_____

_____

_____

_____

_____

_____

_____

_____

_____

_____

We've all been blessed with God-given talents. Mine just happens to be beating people up
– Sugar Ray Leonard
Championship Boxer.

CLUES TO YOUR HIDDEN TALENTS

Chapter 4

Clues to Your Hidden Talents

There are 2 clues to discovering your hidden talents—clues that will reveal your natural strengths. Let's look at the first clue: identifying your true values. In the process of choosing or changing careers, it is important to clarify your beliefs. Values are at the core of beliefs and they can be anything you regard highly—ideas, activities, and things that you prize. If you observe your own activities, you will be able to identify your values because values are what you do, not necessarily what you say.

Because a person has a variety of alternatives on the basis of what he or she values, a clarification of values is extremely crucial to every part of the career decision-making process. If values are not clearly defined, the method of achieving them and the degree of their realization will also be unclear.

True Values

Exercise 1

Values and the Four Heroes

In line with personality preferences, those things you value are consistent with your personality style. Helper values differ from Planner, Thinker, and Doer values. By acknowledging your preferences, you will better understand your own values.

Circle the words that best explain what is important to you.

Helper True Values

Circle the values that you relate to

Authenticity
Being acknowledged
Communication
Compassion

A talent is both a gift and obligation.

It's nice to be important, but it's more important to be nice.

Creativity
Democracy
Emotions
Empathy
Enthusiasm
Friendship
Harmony
Honesty
Individuality
Integrity
Intuition
Love
Natural potential
Optimism
Patience
Peace
Pleasing others
Positive feedback
Public contact
Relationships
Romance
Self–understanding
Sensitivity
Sincerity
Spirituality
Tact
Teamwork
Trustworthiness
Unity

Thinker True Values

Circle the values that you relate to.

Abstraction
Autonomy
Brevity
Cleverness
Competence

Money can't buy love.

A problem is a chance for you to do your best.
–Duke Ellington

Cool-headed under pressure
Creativity
Curiosity
Ethics
Fairness
Focus
Future orientation
Ideas
Imagination
Independence
Ingenuity
Invention
Innovation
Intelligence
Knowledge
Logic
Mental challenge
Objectivity
Precise language
Privacy
Power
Rationality
Self-confidence
Theory
Truth
Vision
Wisdom

Planner True Values

Circle the values that you relate to.

Accuracy
Achievement
Affiliation
Authority
Being meticulous
Caution
Community

If A equals success, then the formula is A equals X plus Y plus Z, where X is work, Y is play, Z is keep your mouth shut.

Is life worth living? This is a question for an embryo, not a man.
-- Samuel Butler

Hard work without talent is a shame, but talent without hard work is a tragedy.
– Robert Half

Compensation
Completion
Conformity
Cooperation
Decisiveness
Dependability
Duty
Efficiency
Facts and data
Family
Justice
Loyalty
Morality
Orderliness
Predictability
Prestige
Profit
Punctuality
Recognition
Religion
Respect
Responsibility
Routine
Rules
Safety
Security
Service
Stability
Status
Structure
Tradition
Wealth

Doer True Values

Circle the values that you relate to.

Action and activity
Adventure

The only way to enjoy anything in life is to earn it first.

Affluence means influence.
– Jack London

Life is ours to be spent, not to be saved.
_ D.H. Lawrence

Aesthetics
Artistic creativity
Camaraderie
Change
Competition
Energy
Entertainment
Excitement
Fast pace
Flexibility
Freedom
Fun
Generosity
Humor
Independence
Optimism
Physical challenge
Playfulness
Pleasure
Profit
Skillfulness
Spontaneity
Variety

Exercise 2

Prioritizing your values

How many values did you circle in each group?

Helper   _____

Thinker   _____

Planner   _____

Doer   _____

Are the totals consistent with the order of your test results? Why or why not?

_____

_____

_____

_____

_____

_____

Exercise 3

Experiencing your values

Our values show through events that happen in our lives. Write about two major life experiences or events that you remember as being special to you.

Major life experience #1

_____

_____

_____

_____

_____

Which values were you demonstrating?

_____

_____

_____

_____

Major life experience #2

_____

_____

_____

_____

_____

_____

Which values were you demonstrating?

_____

_____

_____

_____

Exercise 4

Values Questionnaire

By answering the following questions, you will be able to recognize some of your values.

1. On what have you spent most of your money?

_____

_____

_____

What values can you recognize?

_____

_____

2. Describe a major decision that has made you happy.

_____

_____

_____

What values can you recognize?

_____

_____

3. What is your favorite activity?

_____

_____

What values can you recognize?

_____

_____

4. What would you consider an ideal vacation?

_____

_____

What values can you recognize?

_____

_____

Who are your role models? Name three and briefly discuss what they have in common with you.

1. _____

_____

2. _____

_____

3. _____

_____

What values can you recognize?

_____

_____

Exercise 5

Hobbies

A career may not meet all of your values, but the more of them you meet, the more satisfied you will be. Ensure that your additional values are being satisfied through some area of your life; hobbies are a good outlet for expressing values. List any hobbies you might have.

1.

2.

3.

4.

5.

What values do you recognize through your hobbies?

1.

2.

3.

4.

5.

6.

7.

8.

9.

10.

Exercise 6

Visualize your work environment

Answer these questions to visualize your ideal work environment.

1. Are you working indoors or outdoors?

2. Are you located in one place or are you traveling from one place to another?

3. Do you work alone or with others?

4. Are you working with children or adults?

5. What are you doing that gives you satisfaction?

Think of careers that correspond to this experience and list them below:

1.

2.

3.

4.

5.

Skills

Natural gifts and talents & the 4 primary Heroes

We've established that the first clue to discovering your hidden talents is to identify your true values. Now let's look at the second clue: identifying what you enjoy doing.

We all have an abundance of skills. The question is, which of these skills do we prefer to use in a career? Again, using personality preferences, we can focus on the skills we use naturally and have developed because of preference. An example would be writing with your dominant or preferred hand. You can write with both hands, but you probably write much better with one than the other. When you write with the hand that is dominant, you will do it without struggling and it will flow much better. The same is true when you use your unique gifts and talents. You will experience ease and comfort and therefore, using these skills will seem natural and more enjoyable.

Skills listed in the following Hero groups are the natural gifts and talents for the corresponding personality.

Helper skills

Natural gifts & talents

Your natural gifts are things that you are good at and enjoy doing. Notice how many of these skills involve helping other people, yet they are not specific to only one type of work. These are your transferable skills, which can be used in many diverse occupations. These skills will help you identify work that will give you a sense of passion and fulfillment. Put a star next to the skills you most prefer to use.

Acknowledging others – recognizing and validating others for who they are

Building rapport – bringing harmony to a relationship

Building self-esteem – helping others feel good about themselves

Communicating – effectively exchanging verbal or written information with others

Consulting – giving professional advice

Coordinating – bringing people and activities together in a harmonious way

Counseling – helping others with their personal and professional problems

Enlightening – giving spiritual insight

Expressing feelings – openly communicating feelings with other people

Facilitating groups – assisting a group to harmoniously move in a positive direction

Fostering – nurturing

Guiding others – steering or directing people in a positive direction

Healing – restoring health

Make Love, not war.

Sometimes give your service for nothing ...
– Hippocrates

Helping others – improving the lives of others

Influencing others – having an effect on the lives of other people

Inspiring others – having an exalting influence upon others

Interviewing others – using good communication skills to obtain information from another person

Leading – acting as a positive role model more than being in a position of power or authority

Listening – hearing and paying attention to what others have to say

Mentoring – coaching and supporting others in the direction they want to go

in

Motivating – acting as a catalyst to move others to action

Nurturing – developing and fostering the potential in others

Public speaking – effectively using language to make speeches in public

Recruiting – getting others involved in whatever they believe in

Supporting others – assisting others emotionally

Teaching – enlightening others and motivating them to learn

Training – directing the growth of others

Visualizing – imagining possibilities

Working as a team – bringing a group together to meet a common goal

Thinker skills

Natural gifts & talents

Your natural gifts are things that you are good at and enjoy doing. Notice the emphasis on mental activity, but these skills are not specific to only one type of work. These are your transferable skills, which can be used in many diverse occupations. These skills will help you identify work that will give you a sense of passion and fulfillment. Put a star next to the skills you most prefer to use.

Analyzing – separating or distinguishing the component parts of something to as to discover its true nature or inner relationships

Conceptualizing – forming abstract ideas in the mind

Consulting – giving technical information or providing ideas to define, clarify or sharpen procedures, capabilities, or product specifications

Critiquing – analyzing, evaluating, or appreciating works of art

Curing – restoring to health after a disease

Debating – discussing a question by considering opposing arguments

Designing – mentally conceiving and planning

Developing – making something available to improve a situation

Diagnosing – analyzing the cause or nature of a condition, situation, or problem

Editing – improving and directing publications

Generating ideas – brainstorming or dreaming up ideas

Intellectualizing – using the intellect rather than emotion or experience

Interpreting ideas – explaining the meaning of ideas

The successful people are the ones who think up things for the rest of the world to keep busy at.
– Don Marquis

There may now exist great men for things that do not exist.
Samuel Burchardt

Inventing – developing or creating something for the first time

Learning – gaining knowledge

Observing – examining people, data or things scientifically

Problem solving – identifying key issues or factors in a problem, generating ideas and solutions to solve the problem, selecting the best approach, and testing and evaluating it

Proofreading – reading and marking corrections

Reasoning – thinking

Researching – investigating and experimenting aimed at the discovery and interpretation of facts

Synthesizing – integrating ideas and information

Thinking logically – subjecting ideas to the process of logical thought

Writing – expressing by means of words

Planner skills

Natural gifts & talents

Your natural gifts are things that you are good at and enjoy doing. Notice the emphasis on implementation, but these skills are not specific to only one type of work. These are your transferable skills, which can be used in many diverse occupations. These skills will help you identify work that will give you a sense of passion and fulfillment. Put a star next to the skills you most prefer to use.

Administering policies – managing a course or method of action

Allocating resources – designating resources for a specific purpose

If at first you don't succeed, try reading the instructions.

Attending to detail – paying attention to small items

Bookkeeping – recording the accounts or transactions of a business

Budgeting – planning the amount of money that is available for, required for, or assigned to a particular purpose

Calculating – determining by mathematical means

Caretaking – taking care of the physical needs of others, especially children, the sick and the elderly

Collecting data – gathering information

Coordinating – taking care of logistics for events to flow smoothly

Decision-making – bringing things to a conclusion

Delegating – entrusting responsibilities to other people

Dispatching – sending off or away with promptness

Establishing procedures – constructing a series of steps to be followed in accomplishing something

Estimating cost – judging approximately the value or worth of something

Evaluating – appraising the worth, significance or status of something

Following directions – doing specifically the things told to do by others verbally or in writing

Following through – completing an activity planned or begun

Guarding – protecting or defending

Maintaining schedules – overseeing something designated for a fixed, future

time

Maintaining records – accurate and up-to-date record-keeping

Managing – directing or conducting business or affairs

Monitoring – watching, observing, or checking for a specific purpose

Organizing – arranging things in a systematic order

Paying attention to detail – looking for smaller elements

Planning – making a way of proceeding

Preparing – getting something ready for use or getting ready for some occasion

Recording – putting things in writing

Regulating – governing or directing according to rule or law

Securing – relieving from exposure to danger

Serving – making a contribution to the welfare of others

Supervising – taking responsibility for the work done by others

Doer skills

Natural gifts & talents

Your natural gifts are things that you are good at and enjoy doing. Notice the emphasis on activity, but these skills are not specific to only one type of work. These are your transferable skills, which can be used in many diverse occupations. These skills will help you identify work that will give you a sense of passion and fulfillment. Put a star next to the skills you most prefer to use.

Assembling things – fitting together the parts of things

Either lead, follow, or get out of the way.
– Ted Turner

Coaching – training intensively by instruction, demonstration, and practice

Competing – challenging another for the purpose of winning

Constructing – building something

Dancing – performing rhythmic and patterned bodily movements, usually to music

Displaying things – arranging something in an eye-catching exhibit

Drafting – drawing the preliminary sketch, version, or plan for something

Entertaining – performing publicly for amusement

Gardening – cultivating a plot of ground with herbs, fruits, flowers or vegetables

Illustrating – providing visual features intended to explain or decorate

Influencing others – causing an effect on others

Manipulating – treating or operating with the hands or by mechanical means

Manufacturing – making from raw materials by hand or by machinery

Marketing – planning and strategizing how to present a product or service in the marketplace

Negotiating – conferring with another so as to arrive at the settlement of some matter

Operating tools – skillfully handling tools to perform work

Operating vehicles – driving cabs, limousines, heavy equipment, etc.

Performing – practicing an art that involves public performance

Persuading – influencing others in favor of a product, service, or point of view

Promoting – persuading people to see the value of an idea, person, activity, or cause

Public speaking – expressing yourself before a group

Repairing – restoring by replacing a part or putting together what is torn or broken

Responding to emergencies – being spontaneous and level-headed in emergency situations

Risk taking – having a dangerous element to life

Selling – promoting a service or product with the intent of getting someone to buy or accept it in exchange for something, usually money

Exercise 7

Job Skills

Read through the description above and underline the skills used by a Career Counselor.

Position Title: Career Counselor

Description of duties and responsibilities: Career or vocational counselors help people define their lifestyle, identify skills and aptitudes, develop job hunting skills, select satisfying work and leisure activities. Career counselors use discussion, exercises and tests to determine the client's personality, abilities, interests and values. Then they assist the client in gathering information about career options, evaluating the options, selecting a goal and defining the steps to be taken to reach the goal. They work with clients individually, in groups or in classes. They may keep records of the clients they work with and they must continually keep up with changes in the labor market and be aware of new counseling techniques. They may also help clients write resumes, prepare for interviews and coach them through the job search process. In large companies they may explain career paths or company transfer policies and procedures.

Exercise 8

Create your own job description:

Forget about job titles for a minute. Imagine your ideal occupation/work setting, then write your own job description. Be sure to include the nature of the work: job duties, amount of education or training required, which skills you want to use, the salary and benefits you want, and other important qualities. Make sure you include what you want to spend your day doing and how you want to express yourself.

_____

_____

_____

_____

_____

_____

_____

_____

_____

_____

_____

Underline your true values and skills included in your job description.

Exercise 9

Achievements

Now choose two achievements that you are particular proud of and write a paragraph for each, identifying which skills you were using. Do these skills match the skills listed in your Hero group?

Achievement #1

_____

_____

_____

_____

_____

_____

Underline skills used.

Which are consistent with your Hero group?

_____

_____

_____

_____

Luck is not something you can mention in the presence of self-made men.
– F.B. White

Achievement #2

_____

_____

_____

_____

_____

_____

Underline the skills used.

Which are consistent with your Hero group?

_____

_____

_____

_____

_____

_____

_____

Exercise 10

How do you see me?

Ask another person to describe you. Write their description below.

_____

_____

_____

_____

_____

_____

_____

_____

_____

_____

How is the way that person described you different from how you see yourself?
Why?

_____

_____

_____

_____

_____

_____

_____

_____

_____

_____

What insights have you gained?

_____

_____

_____

_____

_____

_____

_____

LEADERSHIP STYLES

Exercise 11

What kind of leader am I?

Each personality is capable of being a leader, but their style will be different. Your success depends on how consistent your style is with your natural strengths. Write a paragraph discussing a time when you were a leader. What relationship do you see between your natural gifts and talents in Chapter 4 and your leadership style

_____

_____

_____

_____

_____

_____

_____

_____

_____

_____

Exercise 12

Post-test

My first Hero represents my major strengths, the things I do well.
My strengths are:

1.

2.

3.

4.

5.

6.

7.

8.

9.

10.

Judge a leader by the followers.

My last Hero represents my weaknesses, the things I do not do as well.
My weaknesses are:

1.

2.

3.

4.

5.

6.

7.

8.

9.

10.

Capitalize on your strengths; they are most important to use in your work.
Know what you are good at and focus on those areas. Also, understand your
weaknesses in order to manage them. Improve these areas as needed, but with
less emphasis on them in the workplace.

Chapter 4

Short Journal (5 minutes or less)

Your personal strengths are revealed through your values and natural gifts and talents. Describe the difference between your lists of strengths on the pre-test in chapter 1, exercise 1, and what you have discovered about your unique strengths.

_____

_____

_____

_____

_____

_____

_____

_____

_____

_____

Men are created different, they lose their social freedom and their individual autonomy in seeking to become like each other.
–David Reisman

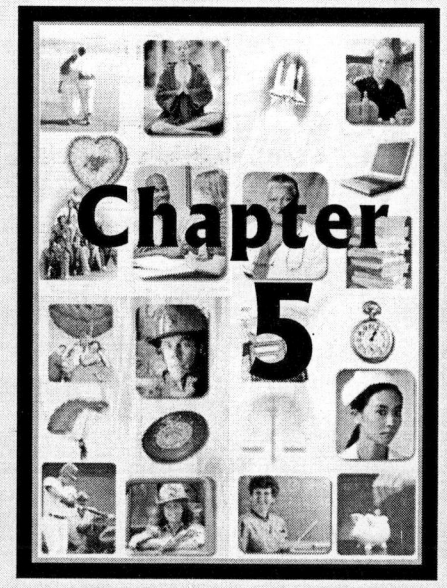

SELF-ESTEEM

Chapter 5

Self-Esteem

Self-esteem is an inside job. It is intrinsic and as natural as breathing. You do not need to do anything other than be who you are to feel good about yourself. You already have what it takes to experience self-esteem, and it belongs to you as your human right.

We have been lead to believe that if we have all the material success we desire, we will feel good about ourselves. In reality, the opposite is true. We only need to be who we are and do what we love in order to have what we desire. If we feel good about ourselves we can have all of those other things. That is why it is so difficult for some people to achieve success—they are doing things in the reverse.

Our self-perceptions drive us in a direction toward success or in a direction away from it. Our natural strengths are our built-in program for self-esteem and success, and it is with these unique gifts and talents that we will begin our examination of career decision-making.

This chapter, as well as subsequent ones, will give you the knowledge you require to begin the road to high self-esteem and success.

Self-Esteeming Characteristics by Hero Group

Let's take a look at the self-esteem characteristics manifest in the four Hero groups.

A man possesses talent; genius possesses the man.
– Issac Stern

Thinker: The Need To Be Mentally Challenged

I feel good about me
    When I ask questions and explore ideas
    When I am open to other people's ideas
    When I work and think independently
    When I need little interaction with others
    When I work and express my creativity
    When I constantly improve my skills
    When I expect much from myself and others

Helper: The Need To Be Real.

I feel good about me
    When I generously show appreciation of others
    When I am honest and sincere
    When I communicate easily with others
    When I use my imagination
    When I express my feelings with enthusiasm
    When I am a Team Player
    When I am feeling peace and harmony

Doer: The Need To Be Free

I feel good about me
    When I am bold and direct
    When I take risks
    When I am spontaneous
    When I am adventurous without drugs
    When I am doing hands-on activities
    When I state things in a direct manner
    When I am very physical

If ignorance is bliss, why aren't more people happy?

Planner: The Need To Be Responsible

I feel good about me
>   When I concentrate on work duties
>   When I am serious
>   When I am helpful to others
>   When I take care of my health and body
>   When I am direct
>   When I follow the rules
>   When I am respectful of others

Exercise 1

What makes me feel good based on what I have learned so far in this workbook.

As a _____ person, I have learned that what makes me feel good about myself is

_____

_____

_____

_____

_____

_____

_____

You are not in competition with anyone but yourself.

_____

_____

_____

_____

_____

Exercise 2

Expressing self-esteem

Understanding yourself and the ways in which you relate to the world will provide opportunities to expand you perspectives. Most importantly, once you recognize those characteristics that are esteeming, you will also develop a compassion for people different than yourself.

Write a brief story about something you have done that made you feel really good about yourself. Take special note of which characteristics from your primary Hero are expressed in the story you relate.

_____

_____

_____

_____

_____

_____

Anything you're good at contributes to happiness.
– Bertrand Russel

It is better to die on your feet than to live on your knees.
– Delores Ibarruri

_____

_____

_____

_____

_____

_____

_____

_____

_____

_____

_____

_____

_____

_____

_____

Self-actualization

Self-actualization is our highest need. We all want to express our true selves and reach our potential, and pursuing your ideal career is a means to doing just that. How you choose to self-actualize is the key. Each Hero is motivated to do this in a different way. The chart below demonstrates how the four personalities choose to reach their potential through self-actualization.

(Based on Maslow's hierarchy of needs)
The Four Paths to Self-Actualization

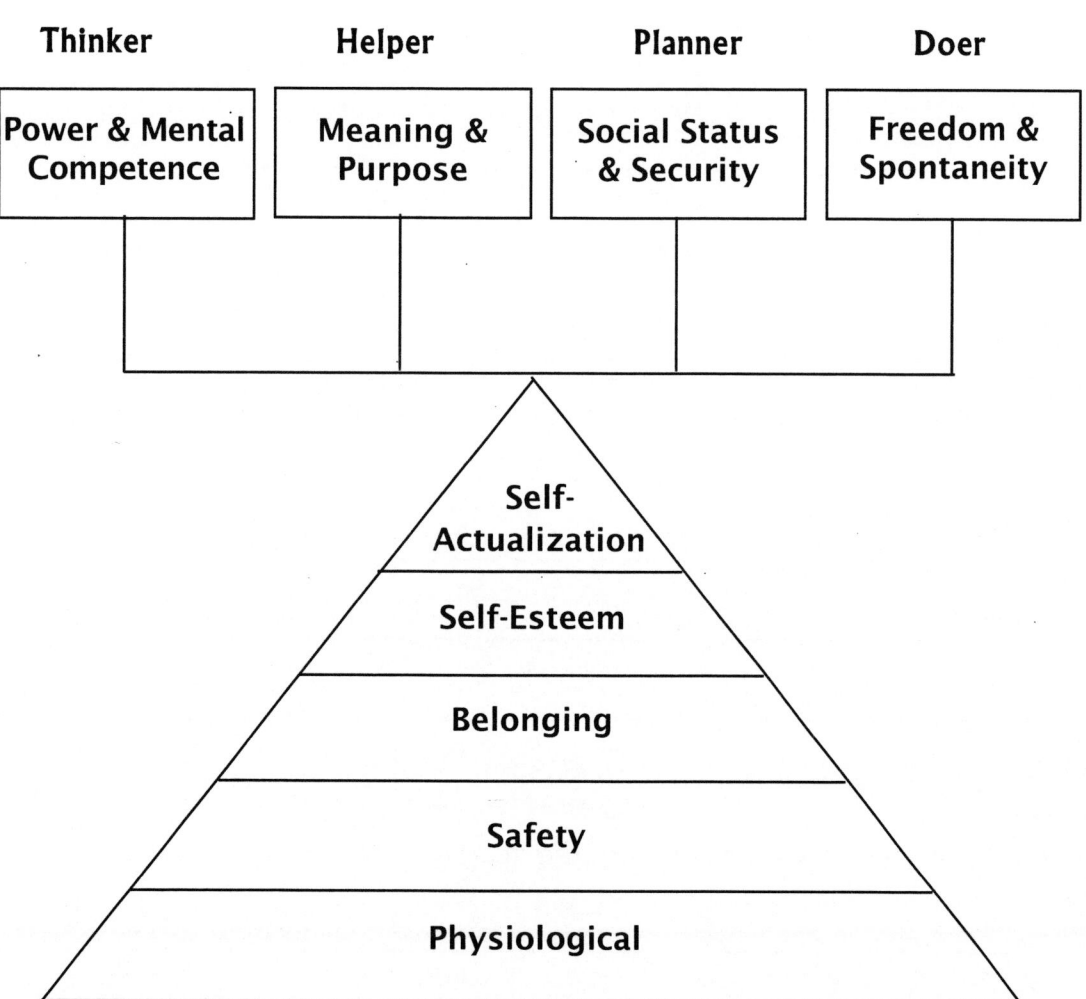

Thinker	Helper	Planner	Doer
Power & Mental Competence	Meaning & Purpose	Social Status & Security	Freedom & Spontaneity

Self-Actualization

Self-Esteem

Belonging

Safety

Physiological

Liberty means responsibility. That is why most men dread it.
Antonio de Mendoza

Exercise 3

Expressing your best self

Choose your primary Hero below, then give an example of when you have felt self-actualized.

If your first Hero is:

Thinker
When have you experienced being powerful or mentally competent?

_____

_____

_____

_____

Helper
When have you experienced feeling meaning and purpose in your life?

_____

_____

_____

_____

Doer
When have you experienced being free and spontaneous?

_____

_____

_____

_____

Planner

When have you experienced having social status and security in your life?

_____

_____

_____

Exercise 4

What Causes You Stress?

Write a one-minute essay about those things that cause stress in your life.

_____

_____

_____

_____

_____

_____

_____

_____

_____

_____

_____

_____

_____

_____

_____

_____

Exercise 5

Stress in my life

List any other stressors you did not write about.

1.

2.

3.

4.

5.

Stress can lead to low self-esteem behavior. We are always striving to feel good about ourselves, but when it can't be done in a positive way it will be done in any way we can. When we suppress our true values it can lead to low self-esteem behavior. Read about this behavior for your Hero group.

What To Look For When You Have Low Self Esteem

There are certain symptoms you can look for when having a bad day—when you are either out or running out of esteem. You can learn to recognize these characteristics, which are generally related to your particular hero grouping.

Thinker

When I feel bad about myself

> I have difficulty making decisions
> I experience lack of cooperation
> I am distant and unsocial
> I become sarcastic and snobbish
> I refuse to communicate ideas
> I need to be perfect based on fear
> I am critical of self and others

Helper

When I feel bad about myself

> I am needy of attention
> I tell lies to look good
> I withdraw
> I space out and daydream
> I cry and feel depressed
> I refuse to obey rules
> I yell and scream

Doer

When I feel bad about myself

I become rude and rebellious
I intentionally break rules
I run away and drop out
I abuse substances
I express acting out behavior
I lie and cheat
I rage and lash out
I procrastinate

Planner

When I feel bad about myself

I complain and feel sorry for myself
I express fear, doubt and worry
I get tired and depressed
I display physical problems caused by emotional stress
I become judgmental
I blindly follow leaders
I become controlling

Exercise 6

Low Self-esteem behavior

Describe a time when you felt low self-esteem:

_____

_____

_____

_____

_____

_____

_____

_____

_____

_____

_____

_____

_____

_____

_____

_____

What caused you to feel this way?

_____

_____

_____

_____

_____

_____

_____

_____

What is the relationship between what triggered your low self-esteem behavior and the things on the list of stressors?

_____

_____

_____

_____

_____

_____

Exercise 7

How to regain self-esteem

What did you do or could have done to regain your self-esteem?

_____

_____

_____

_____

_____

Self-Talk

What are you saying to yourself? Self-talk includes all the thoughts and messages we say to ourselves. It is well documented that what you say about and to yourself affects your mental, emotional and physical well being. Much of this silent, mindless chatter is negative and very destructive. Try to catch yourself when you say things like "I can't pass this class no matter what I do," or "I'm not as smart as _____."

Positive Self-Talk

You can change negative self-talk by reprogramming your mind. It is a matter of training your mind to say positive things to yourself. First you must be aware and listen to how you talk to yourself. Begin to become conscious of this behavior by recording what you say. The use of affirmations is an effective tool to change this inner dialog into positive statements about yourself. An affirmation would be to say, "I can pass this class."

Exercise 8

Negative self-talk

List some of the negative statements you have made to yourself.
Example: I'm not smart enough.

1.

2.

3.

4.

5.

6.

7.

8.

9.

10.

Change each of the negative statements into a positive one (affirmation). Example: I am smart.

1.

2.

3.

4.

5.

6.

7.

8.

9.

10.

Fear

Do you have everything you want in life? If not, why not? Maybe fear is blocking you—fear of failure, fear of success, fear of making the wrong decision. Fear is another barrier to block your creativity and success; it will prevent you from moving forward and giving your best.

Exercise 9

My fears

List those things you are aware of that prevent you from living your dream.
Example: Fear of public speaking

1.

2.

3.

4.

5.

A willingness to face your fear and do whatever it takes to move beyond it is the difference between a successful person and one that gives up. Which do you choose? List ways to turn the above fears around in order to achieve your goals.

Example: Take a public speaking class or hire a speech coach.

1.

2.

3.

4.

5.

Chapter 5

Short Journal (5 minutes or less)

Write a short journal regarding a significant insight you discovered about your-self from reading this chapter.

_____

_____

_____

_____

_____

_____

_____

_____

_____

_____

_____

_____

Keep your talent in the dark and you'll never be insulted.
– Delores Ibarruri

There are two kinds of talents -- man-made talent and God-given talent. With man-made talent you have to work very hard. With God-given talent, you just touch it up once in a while.
-- Pearl Bailey

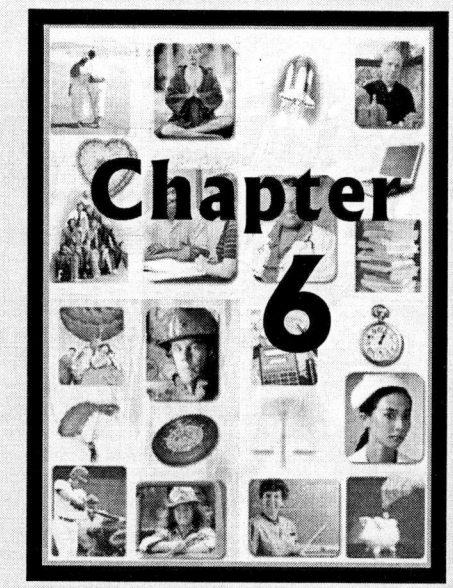

THE FOUR PATHS TO A SUCCESSFUL CAREER

Chapter 6

The Four Paths to a Successful Career

The workplace is constantly changing, and the job that is hot today may not exist by the time you have completed your education or training. Thus, it is not necessarily wise to prepare for one specific occupation.

The most important factor in career decision-making is to know what your strengths are. When you are aware of your unique gifts and talents you are in a strong position to make informed decisions about what you are interested in and what you are good at doing. Your Hero personality traits are key to unlocking these particular strengths and providing information that will give you more options to choose from.

This decision-making process can be approached by choosing either a college major or an occupation that is compatible with your interests and strengths. If you would prefer to begin with a major, think about a subject that you like—one in which you usually get your best grades—since it is important to enjoy the field of study that you choose. Or, you may want to consider a liberal arts major and the many options they offer. Though some worry they won't be able to find work if they are a liberal arts major, today's employers are more concerned about the skills you possess than your major.

It is important to know there is no direct correlation between the degree you choose and the work you will actually do. Studies show that most college graduates are successfully working in fields unrelated to their major. The following examples of three liberal arts majors—history, English and philosophy—show what some people are doing with these degrees.

What liberal arts majors are doing with a degree in:

History
In addition to working for government, politics, and education, history majors are also employed by:

· news departments of local public and commercial radio and TV stations
· newspapers

- history museums
- research and service institutions
- law firms
- firms offering preservation and restoration services
- insurance companies

For more specific career opportunities for History majors, visit the web site: www.uca.edu/history/careers.htm

English
Besides teaching and writing books, English majors are also employed by:
- newspapers
- magazines
- broadcast media—script writing
- trade, professional, or consumer publications
- advertising agencies
- libraries
- bookstores
- radio, TV, movies
- museums
- public relations firms
- corporate legal departments
- commercial bankers

For more specific career opportunities for English majors, visit the web site: www2.uncwil.edu/english/career/htm

Philosophy
In addition to teaching at colleges and universities, philosophy majors are working for:

- research/non-profit organizations
- organizations serving the arts
- religious organizations
- local, national, and international mission fields
- museums
- publishers
- political organizations

- foreign services
- national and state endowments for the Humanities
- consulting services
- public interest research groups

For more specific career opportunities for Philosophy majors, visit the web site: www.udel.edu/apa/index.html#apaonline

Adapted from information prepared by the Career Planning staff at the University of Tennessee.

Here are some more examples of liberal arts majors:

Anthropology
Art History
Biology
Chemistry
Chinese
Economics
French
Geography
German
Italian
Japanese
Mathematics
Physics
Political Science
Psychology
Sociology
Spanish
Speech

Exercise 1

Interesting liberal arts majors

Pick 2 majors and discuss how your own unique interests and strengths relate to each. Use chapter 4 to refresh your memory of your particular talents.

Major #1 _____

_____

_____

_____

_____

_____

Major #2 _____

_____

_____

_____

_____

_____

Exercise 2

Appealing majors

The list below gives examples of majors that appeal to each Hero. Use it for more options, and circle those that appeal to you.

Helper Majors

Elementary education

Secondary education

Special education

Art therapy

Counseling

Child development

Psychology

Rehabilitation counseling

Sociology

Sign Language

Religious studies

Social work

Women's studies

Public relations

Literature

Journalism

Languages

English

Student Personnel Work

Communications

Thinker Majors

Classics

Law

Philosophy

Political Science

Linguistics

Architecture

Medicine

Psychiatry

Computer Science

Engineering

Biology

Veterinary Medicine

Biochemistry

Oceanography

Astronomy

Earth Sciences

Physics

Chemistry

Film making

Planner Majors

Pharmacy

Gerontology

Dentistry

Mathematics

Electrical Engineering

Fish & Wildlife Management

Forestry

Horticulture

Brokerage & Investment

Quality Control

Nursing

Accounting

Banking

City Planning

Legal Assistant

Hotel-Restaurant Management

Finance
Public Health
Economics
Auditing
Library Science

Urban Planning
Hospital Administration
Law Enforcement
Statistics

Doer Majors

Marketing
Fire Science
Auto Mechanics
Air Traffic Control
Construction Engineering
Mining Engineering
Real Estate
Radio & TV
Theater
Media
Physical Education
Music

Physical Education
Art
Design
Interior Design
Physical Therapy
Travel
Music Therapy
Recreation Administration
Cosmetology
Vocational Arts
Dance
Radio & Film Technology

Exercise 3

Universal skills

Regardless of the major you choose, some skills are of universal need in the workplace. It's not enough to only have skills in one focused area. Employers are looking for well-rounded people who can easily adapt to their work environment. Put a check mark next to the following skills you have mastered, and indicate those you need to develop with the letter "I."

Reading ____
Writing ____
Computation ____
Oral communication ____
Creative Thinking/Problem solving   _____
Computer Literacy
Self-esteem _____
Motivation _____

Interpersonal skills ____
Teamwork _____
Leadership _____

Short essay

How do you plan to improve in the areas marked "I"?

_____

_____

_____

_____

_____

_____

_____

_____

_____

_____

_____

_____

CAREER OPTIONS

The second approach to making a good career decision is to look at occupations that will utilize your natural strengths and interests. Forget about job titles and look for work that connects with what you're interested in. Your interests are the things you are curious about and those activities that give you enjoyment and satisfaction. You may think of them as the sum of your values and skills expressed in your reasons for working. This section will help you identify occupations that match your interests.

The following pages list career options that may be of interest to each of the Hero groups. Read all four Hero lists and circle those options of interest to you.

Exercise 1

Careers

Doer

Doer men and women are action oriented. They are highly resourceful and can sell a product, an idea, or a project in a way no other Hero type can. However, their lack of interest in administrative details and follow-through makes them the target of blame and criticism within an organization. When striking out on their own, they must have someone to follow-through if they are to be successful. When the Doer need for excitement and promotional talents are used to constructive ends, any institution is fortunate to have them as employees. However, if these energies are not channeled correctly, destructive and anti-social activities will result. Confining rules and regulations and day-to-day routines are deadly to Doer. Above all else, they seek excitement in a job.

Some examples of careers that you may find interesting are listed below. Remember, you are not limited to these options; refer to the recommended resources to generate additional options.

Circle those that are of interest to you.

Acting Coach
Actor
Advertising Account Executive
Advertising Director
Advertising Sales Representative
Aerospace Assembly Worker
Agricultural Products Sales Representative
Air Safety Inspector
Aircraft Mechanic
Airline Ground Crew
Animal Caretakers and Keeper
Animal Trainer
Animator
Antique Dealer
Apparel Sales Representative
Appliance Repairer
Appraiser
Apprentice
Art Director
Artist
Asbestos Worker
Astronaut
Athletic Coach
Athletic Instructor
Auctioneer
Auto Body and Fender Repairer
Auto Mechanic
Auto Muffler Installer
Auto Stereo and Alarm Installer
Automobile Detailers &Vehicle Cleaner
Automobile Racer
Automobile Salesperson
Automotive Engineer
Automotive Painters
Avionics Technician
Baker
Barber
Bartender
Bath Attendant
Bicycle Repairer
Bindery Worker

Biomedical Equipment Technician
Blacksmiths and Forge Shop Worker
Boat Builder
Boilermaker
Book Illustrators
Booking or Theatrical Agent
Brewmaster
Bricklayer
Broadcast Technician
Building and Construction Inspector
Building Contractor
Building Maintenance Worker
Bus Driver
Business Services Manager
Business Services Salesperson
Buyers and Purchasing Agent
Cabinetmaker
Camera Repairer
Canvasser
Car Rental Agent
Carpenter
Cartoonist
Caterer
Cement Mason
Cemetery Broker
Central Office Installers/Repairer
Chauffeur
Cheesemaker
Chefs and Dinner Cook
Chemical Processing Workers
Chemical Sales Representatives
Child Care Worker
Chimney Sweeps
Chiropractor
Choral Directors
Choreographer
Cinematographer
Civil Engineering Technician
Clown
Coin and Vending Machine Repairer
Color Consultant

Comedian
Commercial Artist
Commercial Fisher
Computer Maintenance Technician
Computer Operator
Computer Sales Representative
Computer Service Technician
Computer Services Sales Representative
Computer Software Training Specialist
Computer Support Specialist
Conservation Worker
Construction Laborer
Consumer Products Dealer
Cosmetologist
Courtesy Grocery Clerk
Crossing Guard
Cruise Director
Dairy Worker
Dance Teacher
Dancer
Day Trader
Delivery Truck Drivers
Demonstrator
Dental Laboratory Technician
Derrick Operator
Diagnostic Medical Sonographer
Diet Technician
Director
Disc Jockey
Dispensing Optician
Diver
Dog Groomer
Domestic Service Worker
Door to Door Salesperson
Drafters
Drilling Representative
Drywall Finisher
Electrician
Electrocardiograph Technician
Electroencephalograph (EEG) Technician
Electro-Mechanical Technician

Electronics Maintenance Technician
Electronics Products Sales Representative
Electronics Technician
Electroplater
Elevator Mechanic
Emergency Medical Technician
Energy Auditor
Event Creation Coordinator
Executive Housekeeper
Extreme Sports Athlete
Farm and Ranch Hand
Farm Equipment Mechanic
Farm Equipment Sales Representative
Farm Machinery Operator
Fashion Illustrator
Fashion Merchandiser
Fashion Model
Fast Food Service Manager
Film Editor
Fingerprint Classifier
Firefighter
Flight Attendant
Floor Covering Installer
Floral Designer
Flying Instructor
Food Processing Worker
Food Product Sales Representative
Food Service Director
Forester
Forestry Technician
Foundry Worker
Free Agent
Freelance Writer
Freight Handler
Fugitive Recovery Agent
Fundraiser
Furniture Mover
Furniture Rental Consultant
Furniture Sales Representative
Furniture Worker

Gamekeeper
Gem Cutter
Gemologist
Glazier
Graphic Design Artist
Grocery Checker
Grounds Manager
Groundskeeper
Gardener
Guide Dog Trainer
Gunsmith
Handcrafter
Hearing Aid Salesperson
Heating and Cooling Systems Mechanic
Heavy Equipment Operator
Helicopter Pilot
Highway Maintenance Worker
Highway Patrol Officer
Horse Trainer
Horseshoer
Horticultural Worker
Hostler (Railroad)
Hotel Desk Clerk
House Mover
Illustrator
Image Consultant
Independent Video Producer
Industrial Arts Teacher
Industrial Designer
Industrial Truck Operator
Innkeeper
Instrument Mechanic
Insulation Installer
Interior Designer
Interior Decorator
Intern
Investment Manager
Iron Fence Erector
Janitor
Jeweler
Jewelry Maker

Jockey
Journalist
Kitchen Helper
Labor Relations Specialist
Landscape Architect
Lather
Laundry and Dry-cleaning Worker
Lifeguard
Light Technician
Line Worker
Lithographic Worker
Lobbyist
Locksmith
Loggers
Longshore Worker
Lumber Graders and Inspectors
Lumber Mill and Plywood Laborers
Machine Tool Operators
Machinist
Magician
Magnetic Resonance Imaging Technologist
Mail Carrier
Maintenance Mechanic
Maitres D'
Marketing Director
Marketing Specialist
Martial Arts Fighter
Massage Technician
Meat Cutter
Mechanical Engineer
Media Relations Executive
Mediator
Merchandise Displayer
Metal Refining Worker
Metallographic Technician
Microfilm Technician
Military Enlisted Personnel
Millwright
Mime
Miner

Mining Engineer
Model Maker
Models
Molder
Motion Picture Producer
Motion Picture Projectionist
Motorcycle Repairer
Music Business Manager
Musical Instrument Maker
Musical Instrument Repairer
Musician
Newspaper Carrier
Nondestructive Testing Engineer
Nuclear Technician
Numerical-Control Machine Operator
Office Machine Repairer
Orchestra Manager
Order Filler
Orthopedist
Outdoor Recreation Planner
Packers and Wrappers
Painter
Paperhanger
Paramedic
Park Ranger
Parts Counter Clerk
Party Planner
Patternmaker
Pawnbroker
Personal Consultant
Pest Control Worker
Petroleum Field Worker
Petroleum Plant Operator
Pharmaceutical Sales Representative
Pharmacy Assistant
Photofinisher
Photographer
Photojournalist
Physical Education Teacher
Physical Therapist
Piano and Organ Tuner

Pilots and Flight Engineer
Plasterers and Drywall Installer
Plastics Fabricator
Plumbers and Pipe Fitters
Podiatrist
Police Officer
Politician
Porters and Bellhops
Press Operator
Producer
Production Painters and Finishers
Production Superintendent
Professional Athlete
Professional Ice Skater
Property Manager
Prosthetists-Orthotists
Public Relations Specialist
Public Speaker
Pulp and Paper Worker
Puppeteer
Race Car Driver
Radio and TV Service Technician
Radio or TV Announcer
Railroad Conductor
Rancher
Real Estate Agent
Real Estate Developer
Recreation Leader
Recreation Program Director
Recreational Therapist
Reducing Salon Attendant
Referees and Umpires
Refuse Collector
Repossessor
Restaurant Consultant
Restaurant Manager
Restoration Specialist
Retail Store Manager
Rigger
Right-of-Way Agent
Robotics Applications Engineer

Robotics Technician
Rock Musicians
Rodeo Performers
Roofers
Rotary Drillers
Roustabouts
Route Salespeople
Sailmaker
Sales and Service Manager
Sales Engineer
Sales Representative
Santa Claus'
Santa's Elves
Saw Filers and Tool Sharpener
Sculptor
Secret Service Agent
Securities Salesperson
Security Guard
Security System Technician
Semiconductor Processor
Service Station Attendant
Service Station Dealer
Set Designer
Scenic Designer
Sheet Metal Worker
Shipfitter
Shipping and Receiving Clerk
Ship's Crew Member
Ship's Officers and Engineer
Ship's Pilot
Shipwright
Shoe Repairer
Shop Iron Worker
Short Order Cook
Sign Language Interpreter
Singer
Ski Lift Operator
Ski Repairer
Small Business Owner
Small Engine Repairer
Snow Ski Instructor

Snowplow Operator
Solar Engineer
Solar System Installer
Sound Engineer
Sound Technician
Special Effects Specialist
Sports General Manager
Sports Medicine Specialist
Sports Nutritionist
Sports Official
Sportscaster
Stage Hand
Stationary Engineer
Stator Rewinder
Steeple Jack
Stock Clerk
Stockbroker
Store Salesperson
Structural Iron Worker
Stunt Performer
Tailors and Garment Fitters
Talent Agent
Talent Manager
Taxi Driver
Technical Illustrator
Telecommunications Services Sales Representative
Telemarketer
Telephone Installers-Repairer
Textile Machine Operator
Theater Manager
Tilesetter
Tire Vulcanizer
Tool and Die Maker
Tow Truck Driver
Traffic Manager
Travel Agent
Travel Consultant
Tree Surgeon
Tree Trimmer
Trial Lawyer

Truck and Heavy Equipment Mechanic
Truck Driver
Turfgrass Manager
Upholsterer
Vehicle Washers and Equipment Cleaners
Vendor
Videographer
Voice-Over Artist
Waiter or Waitress
Wardrobe Supervisor
Warehouse Worker
Watch Repairer
Water and Wastewater Plant Operators
Water Well Driller
Wedding Consultant
Weights and Measures Technicians
Welder
Woodworking Machine Operator
X-Ray Technician

Planner

Planner persons are realistic, matter-of-fact, and more curious about new products than they are about new ideas and theories. They are very good at following procedures and in detailing rules and regulations. They prefer work environments in which duties and authorities are well-defined, and where they can be rewarded through hard work and feel valued as responsible and dependable employees. Their interest in thoroughness, pragmatism, punctuality, and efficiency leads them to occupations in which these preferences are appreciated.

Some examples of careers that you may find interesting are listed below. Remember, you are not limited to these options; refer to the recommended resources to generate additional options.

Circle those that are of interest to you.

Accountant	Cashier
Accounting Clerk	Casino Dealer
Administrative Assistant	Census Enumerator
Agricultural Inspector	Certified Public Accountant
Air Traffic Controller	City Manager
Airport Manager	Claims Clerk
Apartment House Manager	Clerk Typist
Archivist and Curator	Closet Organizer
Association Executive	Clothing Patternmaker
Auditor	Coin Machine Collector
Automobile Assembler	Collection Agent
Automobile Contract Clerk	Collection Worker
Bailiff	Compositor
Bank Officer	Computer Operator
Bank Operations Officer	Computer Programmer
Bank Teller	Computer Security Specialist
Beekeeper	Contract Administrator
Blood Bank Specialist	Corporate Accountant
Bookkeeper	Corporate Lawyer
Border Patrol Agent	Corrections Officer
Budget Analyst	Counter Attendant
Business Teacher	Court Clerk
Cannery and Frozen Food Worker	Court Interpreter
Career Information Technician	Court Reporter
Cartographer	Credit Analyst

Credit Manager
Credit Worker
Customs Canine Specialist
Customs Inspector
Data Entry Operator
Dental Assistant
Dental Hygienist
Dentist
Deportation Officer
Dining Room Attendant
Dispatcher
Drawbridge Operator
Driving Instructors
Economist
EDP Auditor
Education Administrator
Electrologist
Electronics Production Worker
Elementary School Teacher
Enologist
Escrow Officer
Estimator
Executive Secretary
Expediter
Farm Labor Contractor
Farmers and Farm Manager
File Clerk
Financial Planner
Fish and Game Warden
Food and Drug Specialist
Food Service Manager
Foreign Service Officers
Forester
Front Office Managers
Funeral Directors and Embalmers
General Office Clerk
Geneticist
Geriatric Care Manager
Gerontologists
Golf Club Manager
Health and Safety Inspector
Health Service Administrator

History Teacher
Home Economist
Hospital Administrator
Hospital Central Supply Technician
Hotel and Restaurant Manager
Houseparent
Human Resource Manager
Immigration Inspector
Industrial Engineer
Information Abstractors and Indexers
Insurance Adjuster
Insurance Agent
Insurance Clerk
Insurance Salesperson
Interviewing Clerk
Investor Relations Executive
Judge
Law Enforcement Officer
Law Office Manager
Legal Assistant
Legal Secretary
Legislative Aide
Librarian
Library Assistant (Clerical)
Library Technician
Licensed Vocational Nurse
Loan Officer
Lodging Manager
Mail Clerk
Math Teacher
Medical Assistant
Medical Billing Service
Medical Doctor
Medical Records Administrator
Medical Records Technician
Medical Secretary
Medical Transcriptionist
Messenger
Meter Reader
Military Officer
Mortgage Broker
Municipal Clerk

New Account Clerk
Nuclear Medicine Technologist
Nun
Nurse
Nurse Midwife
Nurse Practitioner
Nursing Assistant
Nursing Director
Occupational Therapist
Occupational Therapy Assistant
Office Machine Operator
Office Manager
Order Clerk
Paralegal/Legal Assistant
Parking Lot Attendant
Parole and Probation Officers
Patient Account Representative
Payroll Clerk
Peripheral EDP Equipment Operator
Personnel Assistants and Clerk
Pharmacist
Physical Therapist
Physical Therapy Assistant
Picture Framer
Podiatric Assistant
Police Officer
Polygraph Examiner
Postal Clerk
Postmaster
Product Manager
Production Clerk
Production Planner
Production Worker
Proofreader
Property Manager
Psychiatric Technician
Public Administrator
Public Health Educator
Public Health Nurse
Radiologic Technologist
Radiology Technician
Railroad Brake Operator

Real Estate Agent or Broker
Real Estate Broker
Receptionist
Receptionists and Information Clerks
Records Clerk
Records Manager
Recreational Therapist
Registered Nurse
Rental Clerk
Reservation Manager
Respiratory Therapist
Reunion Planner
Room Cleaner
School Administrator
School Counselor
Secretary
Securities Clerk
Sewing Machine Operator
Shorthand Reporter
Special Events Planner
Statistical Clerk
Statistical Clerk
Statistician
Stenographer
Survey Interviewer
Tape Librarian
Tax Examiner
Tax Preparer
Telephone Operator
Ticket and Reservations Agent
Title Examiner
Toll Collector
Traffic Rate Clerk
Transportation Planner
Typesetter
U.S. Marshall
Underwriter
Union Business Representative
Urban Planner
Ward Clerk
Word Processing Machine Operator

Thinker

Thinkers are the most reluctant of all the Hero types to do things in a traditional manner. They are always on the lookout for new projects, new activities, and new procedures. This accounts for their tendency to become entrepreneurs and to work for themselves. Thinkers can succeed in a variety of occupations as long as the job does not involve too much hum-drum routine. They tend to lose interest once their work is no longer challenging and they may fail to follow-through, often to the discomfort of colleagues. As an employee, the Thinker might work against the system just for the joy of being one-up. However, this type can contribute immensely in a work atmosphere that allows independence and expression of ingenuity.

Some examples of careers that you may find interesting are listed below. Remember, you are not limited to these options; refer to the recommended resources to generate additional options.

Circle those that are of interest to you.

Actor	Art Gallery Owner
Actuary	Artist
Acupressurist	Astronomer
Acupuncturist	Astrophysicist
Administrative Hearing Interpreter	Automobile Designer
Advertising Executive	Biochemist
Aerospace Engineer	Biologist
Agricultural Engineer	Biomedical Engineer
Agricultural Scientist	Biomedical Researcher
Agronomist	Book Publisher
Air Traffic Controller	Botanist
Anesthesiologist	Brand Manager
Animal Health Technician	Business Executive and Manager
Animal Scientist	Business Planner
Anthropologist	Business Programmer
Aquaculturist	Calibration Technician
Archaeologist	Cardiologist
Architect	CAT Technologist
Arson Investigator	Central Intelligence Agent
Art Advisor	Ceramic Engineer
Art Critic	Chemical Engineer

Chemical Laboratory Technician
Chemist
Chiropractor
Civil Engineer
College Professor/Researcher
Columnist
Community Organization Worker
Compensation Analyst
Computer Consultant
Computer Engineer
Computer Graphics Specialist
Computer Operations Manager
Computer Programmer Aide
Computer Programmer
Computer Scientist
Computer Security Specialist
Computer Systems Analyst
Consultant
Copy Editor
Copywriter
Coroner
Corrosion Engineer
Crime Laboratory Technician
Criminal Lawyer
Criminologist
Cryptanalyst
Curator
Dairy Scientist
Data Base Manager
Debater
Dentist
Dermatologist
Design Engineer
Desktop Publisher
Detective and Investigator
Dialysis Technician
Documentation Specialist
Ecologist
Economists
Editor

Elected Official
Electrical and Electronics Engineer
Electrical and Electronics Technician
Electron Microscopists
Electro-Optical Engineer
Engineer
Engineering and Science Manager
Engineering Technician
Entomologist
Environmental Analyst
Environmental Engineer
Epidemiologist
FBI Agent
Fiber-Optic Engineers and Technician
Film Critic
Financial Analyst
Fire Protection Engineer
Fish and Wildlife Specialist
Fish Pathologist
Food Technologists and Scientist
Games Programmer
Genealogist
Genetic Engineer
Geologic Technician
Geologist
Geophysicist
Ghost Writer
Grant Writer
Graphic Artist
Graphic Artist and Designer
Handwriting Analyst
Hazardous Materials Technician
Hazardous Waste Manager
Hearing Officer
Histotechnologist
Home-Based Worker
Horse Management Worker
Horticulturist
Human Factors Engineer
Hydrologists

Industrial Designer
Industrial Engineering Technician
Industrial Relations Director
Information Broker
Information Researcher
Information Resource Manager
Instrumentation Technician
Internet Project Manager
Internist (Physicians)
Interpreters and Translator
Inventor
Job Analyst
Journalist
Judge
Labor Relations Specialist
Laser Technician
Law Clerk
Lawyer
Lecturer
Liberal Arts Teacher
Literary Agent
Lyricist
Management Consultant
Manufacturing Engineer
Marine Biologist
Market Researcher
Math Teacher
Mathematician
Mathematics and Science Teacher
Mechanical Engineering Technician
Medical Doctor
Medical Laboratory Assistant
Medical Laboratory Technician
Medical Researcher
Medical Technologist
Metallurgical Engineer
Meteorologist
Microbiologist
Microwave Technician
MIS Manager

Motion Picture Director
Motion Picture Producer
Movie Critic
Multimedia Occupations
Naval Architect
Network Control Technician
Network Managers and Administrator
Network Specialist
News Writer
Newspaper Editor
Nondestructive Tester
Nuclear Engineer
Nuclear Medicine Technologist
Numerical Control Tool Programmer
Nurse Anesthetist
Oceanographer
On-Line Multimedia Content Developer
Operations and Systems Researcher
Operations Research Analyst
Ophthalmologist
Optical Technician
Optometrist
Osteopath
Paleontologist
Paralegals and Legal Assistant
Parapsychologist
Pathologist
Perfusionist
Personal Computer Programmer
Petroleum Engineer
Photographer
Photonic Technician
Physical Therapist
Physician's Assistant
Physicians
Plastics Engineer
Playwright
Podiatrist
Policy Analyst
Political Scientists

Private Investigator
Project Manager
Psychiatrist
Psychologist
Public Health Microbiologist
Quality Control Inspector
Quality Engineer
Radiation Safety Technician
Radio and Television Broadcaster
Radiologist
Railroad Engineer
Range Manager
Rehabilitative Engineer
Risk Resolver
Safety Engineer
Sanitary Engineer
Science Teacher
Science Technician
Scientific Programmer
Screen Writer
Scriptwriter
Seismologist
Social Scientist
Software Engineer
Software Programmer
Soil Engineer
Soil Scientist
Speech Pathologist
Speech Writer
Statistician
Stockbroker
Surgeon
Surgical Technician
Surveying and Mapping Technician
Surveyors and Mapping Scientist
Systems Analyst
Systems Programmer
Taxidermist
Team Leader
Technical Writer

Technical Writers and Editor
Telecommunications Analyst
Telecommunications Engineer
Telecommunications Programmer Analyst
Telecommunications Technicians
Telecommuter
Test Engineer
Textbook Writer
Time-Study Analyst
Traffic Technician
Transportation Engineer
Treasury Enforcement Agent
University and College Teacher
Urban and Regional Planner
Veterinarian
Viticulturist
Volcanologist
Web Developer
Webmaster
Writer, Fiction
Writer, Science Fiction Book

Helper

Helpers have a remarkable latitude in career choices and they succeed in many fields. They are imaginative, enthusiastic, and can do almost anything which is of interest to them. At work, they are at ease with colleagues, and others enjoy their presence. They are highly creative in dealing with people and are outstanding at inspiring group spirit and getting people together. Helpers are likely to lose interest in their job once people or projects become routine. They prefer a family-like, friendly, personalized, and warm work environment. They dislike jobs which require painstaking detail and follow-through over a period of time. They prefer people-oriented careers and job opportunities which allow creativity and variety in day-to-day operations.

Some examples of careers that you may find interesting are listed below. Remember, you are not limited to these options; refer to the recommended resources for additional options.

Circle those that are of interest to you.

Actor
Aerobics Teacher
Airbrush Artist
Airline Receptionist
Alcohol and Drug Treatment Counselor
Animal Control Workers
Animal Trainers
Announcer, TV
Art Teacher
Art Therapist
Audiologist
Bilingual School Teacher
CalWORKS Counselor
Career Coach
Career Counselor
Case Worker
Caseworker Supervisor
Child Care Worker
Child Development Teacher
Choral Director
Choreographer
Clergy

Clinical Psychologist
Clothes Designers
Color Consultant
Columnist/Commentator
Community Affairs Coordinator
Community Affairs Representative
Community Relations Advisor
Coordinator, Rehab. Service
Coordinator, Volunteer Service
Copy Writer
Cosmetologist
Costumer
Counseling Psychologist
Creative Writer
Customer Service Representative
Dance Teacher
Dancer
Dean of Student
Demonstrators and Product Promoter
Dental Assistant
Developmental Psychologist
Dietitians and Nutritionist
Director of Guidance, Public Schools

Director of Student Affairs
Director, Commission for the Blind
Director, Educational Program
Director, Educational, Health
Director, Preschool
Director, Religious Education
Director, Special Education
Director, Vocational Training
Display Designer
Drama Teacher
Dramatic Coach
Editor, Magazine
Editorial Writer
Education Consultant
Education Program Specialist
Educational Therapist
Elementary School Teacher
Employee Development Specialist
Employment Interviewer
English Teacher
Faculty Member
Family Child Care Provider
Family Lawyer
Family Practitioner
Fashion Artist
Fashion Designer
Fashion Editor
Fashion Model
Fashion Writer
Flight Attendant
Floral Designer
Foreign Language Interpreter
Foreign Language Teacher
Foreign Language Translator
Foreign Student Advisor
Fund-raiser
Genealogist
General Practitioner
Genetic Counselor
Gerontology

Graduate Teaching Assistant
Greeting Card Writer
Gynecologist
Hat Designer
Health Educator
Health Therapist
Home Health Aide
Home Schooling Consultant
Home Tutor
Hotel Desk Clerk
Human Services Worker
Hypnotherapist
Illustrator
Impersonator
In-Home Health Care Provider
Instructional Coordinators
Instructor, Extension Work
Instructor, Modeling
Instructor, Vocational Training
Interior Designer
Jeweler
Journalist
Lawyer for Battered Women
Life Coach
Magician
Makeup Artists
Manager, Department Store
Manager, Education and Training
Manager, Employee Welfare
Manager, Employment
Manicurist
Marketing Communication Expert
Marriage & Family Therapist
Massage Therapist
Medical Social Worker
Mental Health Counselor
Merchandise Displayers
Metaphysical Practitioner
Metaphysical Teacher
Mime
Minister/Rabbi

Model
Motivational Speaker
Music Teacher
Nannies
Naturopathic Doctor
News Reporter
Newscaster
Nun
Nursing Educator
Nutrition and Weight Loss Instructor
Obstetricians and Gynecologists
Occupational Therapist
Occupational Therapist Aide
Painter
Pastoral Counselor
Pediatrician
Pedicurist
Personal Coach
Personnel Agency Manager
Personnel Recruiter
Playwright
Poet
Preschool Teacher
Professor, Women's Studies
Prothetists
Psychiatric Aide
Psychiatric Social Worker
Psychic Reader
Psychodramatist
Psychologist
Psychology Teacher, Post Secondary
Public Health Educator
Public Relations Specialist
Public Relations Worker
Puppeteer
Radio Announcer
Receptionists and Information Clerk
Recreation Leader
Recreational Therapist
Recreational Worker

Recruiter
Rehabilitation Counselor
Reporters
Residence Counselor
Respiratory Therapist
School Counselor
School Nurse
School Psychologist
Script Writer
Secondary School Teachers
Shoe Designer
Sign Language Interpreter
Singer
Skin Care Specialist
Social and Community Service Managers
Social Director
Social Program Planner
Social Science Teacher
Social Scientist
Social Service Aide
Social Worker
Sociologist
Sociology Teacher, Postsecondary
Special Education Teacher
Speech Coach
Speech Pathologist
Spiritual Counselor
Story Editor
Student Personnel Work
Substance Abuse Social Worker
Sculptor
Talent Director
Talk Show Host/Hostess
Teacher Aide
Teacher, Adult Education
Teacher, Blind
Teacher, Deaf
Teacher, Disabled
Teacher, Elementary

Teacher, Mentally Retarded
Team Building Consultant
Tour Guide
Trainer
Training and Development Specialist
Travel Agent
Tutor
Usher
Vocational Education Teacher
Vocational-Rehabilitation Counselor
Wardrobe Consultant
Wedding Consultant
Weight Loss Counselor
Welfare Director
Writer, Children's Books
Writer, Non-Fiction Books
Writer, Romance Novels
Writer, Prose, Fiction
Writer, Technical
Yoga Teacher

Discover more career options with the World of Work Map!

About the Map

- The map arranges job families (groups of similar jobs) into 12 regions. Together, the job families cover all U.S. jobs.

- A job family's location is based on its primary work tasks—working with DATA, IDEAS, PEOPLE, and THINGS.

- To use the map, find the job families in line with the work tasks you prefer. Then find out about the jobs in those job families.

· Heroes: Helper, Thinker, Planner, Doer.

· Holland Themes: (A) Artistic; (I) Investigative; (R) Realistic;
  (C) Conventional; (S) Social; (E) Enterprising
· Temperament Types: NF=Helper; NT= Thinker; SP=Doer; SJ= Planner

The map contains job groupings arranged by regions and work tasks.
(Refer to the list on the following two pages.)

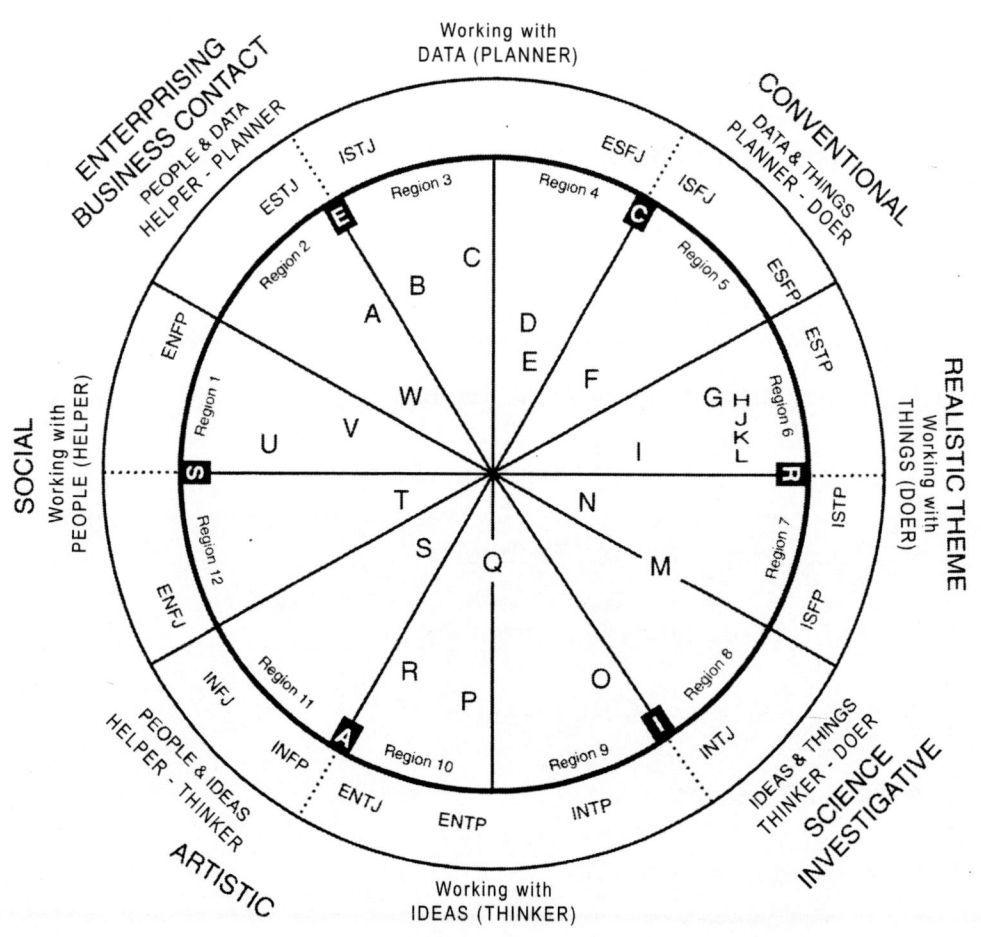

Legend

PLANNER

A. Marketing & Sales

B. Management & Planning

C. Records & Communication

D. Financial Transactions

E. Storage & Dispatching

F. Business Machine/Computer Operation

DOER

G. Vehicle Operation & Repair

H. Construction & Maintenance

I. Agriculture & Natural Resources

J. Crafts & Related Services

K. Home/Business Equipment Repair

L. Industrial Equipment Operation & Repair

THINKER

M. Engineering & Related Technologies

N. Medical Specialties & Technologies

O. Natural Sciences & Mathematics

P. Social Sciences

Q. Applied Arts (Visual)

R. Creative/Performing Arts

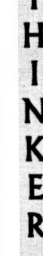

**H
E
L
P
E
R**

S. Applied Arts (Written & Spoken)

T. General Health Care

U. Education & Related Services

V. Social & Government Services

W. Personal/Customer Services

How to Find Your Career Options

Do you enjoy working with:

PEOPLE (Helper)—People you help, care for, or sell things to? See regions 12 and 1.

DATA (Planner)—Facts, numbers, files, business procedures? See regions 3 and 4.

THINGS (Doer)—Machines, tools, living things? See regions 6 and 7.

IDEAS (Thinker)—Using words, equations, or music? See regions 9 and 10.

This map is based on the research of The American College Testing Program -- Career Planning Services (© 1984).

Exercise 2

World of Work Map

Using the World of Work Map, locate your primary job family. Look for career options below that are within your particular group, and circle those that interest you.

DATA (PLANNER)

Travel agents
Insurance agents
Wholesalers
Office supply sales workers
Buyers
Purchasing agents

Small business owners
Receptionist
Office messengers
Word processor
Grocery check-out clerk
Hotel clerks
Payroll clerk
Dental assistants
Hospital attendants
Bookkeeping computer operator
Postal inspector
Plant nursery worker

PEOPLE (HELPER)

Newswriters
Reporters
Fashion Designers
Commercial Artists
Interior Decorators
Nightclub entertainers
Popular musicians
Recreation workers

THINGS (DOER)

Barber
Tailor
Shoemaker
Butcher
Baker
Cook
Rancher
Pet shop attendant
Sheet metal worker
Bricklayer
Bulldozer operator
Crane operator
Electrician
Printing press operator
Draftsmen
Pilot

IDEAS (THINKER)
Medical technologist
Lab worker
Biologist
Ecologist
Statistician
Agricultural scientist
Author
Concert singer

Heroes equivalents to other personality systems that provide career information

D.O.T—Dictionary of Occupational Titles

Data	Planner
People	Helper
Things	Doer
Ideas	Thinker

HOLLAND THEMES—The Strong Campbell Interest Inventory

Realistic	Doer, Planner
Artistic	Helper, Thinker, Doer
Investigative	Thinker
Social	Helper
Enterprising	Doer, Thinker
Conventional	Planner

Keirsey—"Please Understand Me"

NF	Helper
NT	Thinker
SJ	Planner
SP	Doer

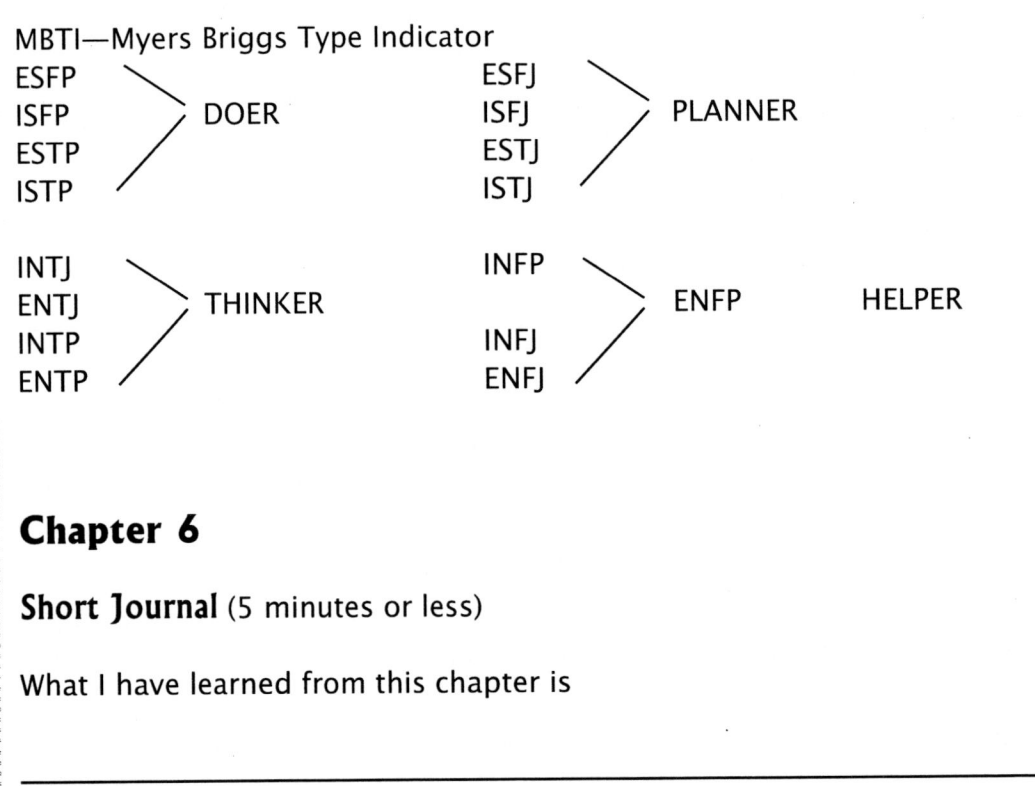

MBTI—Myers Briggs Type Indicator

ESFP
ISFP   DOER
ESTP
ISTP

ESFJ
ISFJ   PLANNER
ESTJ
ISTJ

INTJ
ENTJ   THINKER
INTP
ENTP

INFP
          ENFP   HELPER
INFJ
ENFJ

Chapter 6

Short Journal (5 minutes or less)

What I have learned from this chapter is

_____

_____

_____

_____

_____

_____

_____

The only place where success comes before work is in a dictionary.
-- Vidal Sassoon.

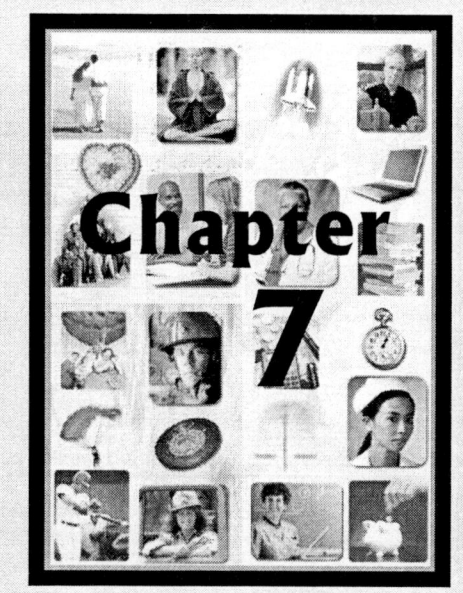

Chapter 7

RESEARCH

Chapter 7

Research

How To Obtain Information About Career Options

Good decisions cannot be made without information. It is time to gather information about your top career choices in order to decide which will be most fulfilling. In addition to learning the values and skills needed for each option, you will need to know such things as duties, education/training, and salary.

You may use any of the following, as well as resources found in most libraries and college career centers, to do your research.

1. The Dictionary of Occupational Titles (DOT) lists over 20,000 different career titles.   A job description is given with skills required for each occupation.

2. The O*NET—Occupational Information Network is a computer database designed to combine the DOT and OOH. See http://online.onetcenter.org.

You may want to check out these career assessment web sites:

1. www.innerheroes.com

This site offers information about the book **Follow Your Inner Hero to the Work You Love.**

2. www.keirsey.com

This site offers The Keirsey Character Sorter and The Keirsey Temperament Sorter based on the Myers-Briggs personality types.

3. www.self-directed-search.com

A career assessment based on the Self-Directed Search.

4. www.jobhuntersbible.com/counseling

Career centers usually will have this resource system.

EUREKA is a California career information system that delivers occupational and educational information on 390 occupations, 140 programs of study and training, 221 post-secondary schools in California, and more than 1,700 colleges and universities in the United States.

Exercise 1

Worksheets

Use the following career research worksheets to answer questions about each of your 5 or more options.

CAREER RESEARCH WORKSHEET

Position title: _____

Description of duties and responsibilities:

_____

_____

_____

Where to look for this type of career:

_____

_____

Education, training, or experience required:

_____

_____

_____

Beneficial personal qualities:

_____

_____

_____

Expected earnings: _____

Immediate outlook for this career (1–5 years):

_____

_____

_____

Long-term outlook (5–10 years):

_____

_____

_____

Sources and references:

_____

_____

_____

CAREER RESEARCH WORKSHEET

Position title: _____

Description of duties and responsibilities:

_____

_____

_____

Where to look for this type of career:

_____

_____

Education, training, or experience required:

_____

_____

_____

_____

Beneficial personal qualities:

_____

_____

Expected earnings: _____

Immediate outlook for this career (1–5 years):

_____

_____

_____

_____

Long-term outlook (5–10 years):

_____

_____

_____

_____

Sources and references:

_____

_____

_____

_____

CAREER RESEARCH WORKSHEET

Position title: _____

Description of duties and responsibilities:

_____

_____

_____

Where to look for this type of career:

_____

_____

Education, training, or experience required:

_____

_____

_____

_____

Beneficial personal qualities:

_____

_____

Expected earnings: _____

Immediate outlook for this career (1–5 years):

_____

_____

_____

_____

Long-term outlook (5–10 years):

_____

_____

_____

_____

Sources and references:

_____

_____

_____

_____

_____

CAREER RESEARCH WORKSHEET

Position title: _____

Description of duties and responsibilities:

_____

_____

_____

Where to look for this type of career:

_____

_____

Education, training, or experience required:

_____

_____

_____

_____

Beneficial personal qualities:

_____

_____

Expected earnings: _____

Immediate outlook for this career (1–5 years):

_____

_____

_____

_____

Long-term outlook (5–10 years):

_____

_____

_____

_____

Sources and references:

_____

_____

_____

_____

CAREER RESEARCH WORKSHEET

Position title: _____

Description of duties and responsibilities:

_____

_____

_____

Where to look for this type of career:

_____

_____

Education, training, or experience required:

_____

_____

_____

_____

Beneficial personal qualities:

_____

_____

Expected earnings: _____.

Immediate outlook for this career (1–5 years):

_____

_____

_____

_____

Long-term outlook (5–10 years):

_____

_____

_____

_____

Sources and references:

_____

_____

_____

_____

_____

CAREER RESEARCH WORKSHEET

Position title: _____

Description of duties and responsibilities:

_____

_____

_____

Where to look for this type of career:

_____

_____

Education, training, or experience required:

_____

_____

_____

_____

Beneficial personal qualities:

_____

_____

Expected earnings: _____

Immediate outlook for this career (1–5 years):

_____

_____

_____

_____

Long-term outlook (5–10 years):

_____

_____

_____

_____

Sources and references:

_____

_____

_____

_____

_____

TYING IT ALL TOGETHER

The information provided should have given some options to help make a decision about the direction you want to take in your career. To experience satisfaction in your work it is important to be who you are by expressing your true values, and do what you love by using your best skills. Your career decision could eventually lead to your life's work—your ultimate career. The exercise below will help you evaluate your choices and clarify their soundness.

Exercise 2

Clarifying your values, skills, and occupations

Your values clarify how you need to express yourself in your work. List 5 or more of your most important values from chapter 4.

1. _____

2. _____

3. _____

4. _____

5. _____

6. _____

7. _____

When you are able to use your best skills, you enjoy what you do. List 5 or more of your most enjoyable skills from chapter 4.

1. _____

2. _____

3. _____

4. _____

5. _____

6. _____

7. _____

List 5 of the top career choices from your completed research sheets.

1. _____

2. _____

3. _____

4. _____

5. _____

6. _____

7. _____

Exercise 3

Career Summary

Complete one of the following sheets for each of your 5 career choices.
If you cannot provide the requested information, maybe you need to consider other options more related to your values and skills.

Career #1 _____

List the values you will express in this work.

_____

_____

_____

_____

_____

_____

Explain how you will express each value.

_____

_____

_____

_____

_____

_____

_____

List the skills you will use in this work.

_____

_____

_____

_____

_____

_____

_____

Explain how you will use each skill.

_____

_____

_____

_____

_____

_____

_____

_____

Career #2 _____

List the values you will express in this work.

_____

_____

_____

_____

_____

_____

Explain how you will express each value.

_____

_____

_____

_____

_____

_____

_____

List the skills you will use in this work.

_____

_____

_____

_____

_____

_____

Explain how you will use each skill.

_____

_____

_____

_____

_____

_____

_____

Career #3 _____

List the values you will express in this work.

_____

_____

_____

_____

_____

_____

Explain how you will express each value.

_____

_____

_____

_____

_____

_____

_____

List the skills you will use in this work.

_____

_____

_____

_____

_____

_____

_____

Explain how you will use each skill.

_____

_____

_____

_____

_____

_____

_____

Career #4 _____

List the values you will express in this work.

_____

_____

_____

_____

_____

_____

Explain how you will express each value.

_____

_____

_____

_____

_____

_____

_____

List the skills you will use in this work.

_____

_____

_____

_____

_____

_____

Explain how you will use each skill.

_____

_____

_____

_____

_____

_____

Career #5 _____

List the values you will express in this work.

_____

_____

_____

_____

_____

_____

Explain how you will express each value.

_____

_____

_____

_____

_____

_____

_____

List the skills you will use in this work.

_____

_____

_____

_____

_____

_____

_____

Explain how you will use each skill.

_____

_____

_____

_____

_____

_____

_____

Chapter 7

Short Journal (5 minutes or less)

What I have learned about myself in this chapter is

_____

_____

_____

_____

_____

_____

_____

_____

_____

_____

_____

_____

_____

_____

_____

_____

_____

_____

_____

_____

_____

_____

_____

_____

_____

_____

_____

_____

_____

_____

Knowledge is of two kinds. We know a subject ourselves, or we know where we can find information upon it.
– Samuel Johnson

INFORMATIONAL INTERVIEWING

Chapter 8

Informational Interviewing

What is an informational interview?

An informational interview is a great way to gather information from an expert in a particular field. It is the simple method of talking with someone about their area of work, and asking questions about how they got started and what it's like to do the work they do. All it requires is for you to ask questions—let the other person do most of the talking.

How do I interview someone for information?

You are now ready to choose one of the occupations you have researched and talk to someone who works in that field about what the job is really like on a day-to-day basis. This is also called "networking." Be sure your contacts understand that the purpose of these interviews is not to find a job, but to gather personal information regarding the occupation or profession. Most people love to talk about their work.

Use the computer, career files and directories, instructors, and friends or relatives to assist you in locating local organizations in the fields of your interest. Call for an appointment with the appropriate person or ask the personnel department to suggest someone.

As you go through this exercise, remember that you are seeking a career that is esteeming to you; be alert for those characteristics of the work environment and personnel that will identify specific hero traits. It is important to your future that your values and your natural skills and talents be compatible with your work.

Ask to interview the person at their place of employment. This will provide an opportunity for you to observe the working environment. And remember the following:

- Make a good impression—you may want to return to request employment.
- Be on time and dress appropriately.
- If you must cancel or reschedule the appointment, call to let them know.

- Take notes during the interview and ask questions.
- Ask for a business card.
- Send a thank-you note for the person's time and assistance.

Exercise 1

Interview questions

Answer the following questions about each interview.

1. Date and time of interview: _____

2. Name and job title of person interviewed: _____

3. Description of a typical workday: _____

_____

_____

_____

4. Qualifications for job:_____

_____

_____

5. How did this person break into this field? _____

_____

_____

6. What is the job market like?_____

_____

_____

_____

7. What are starting salaries? _____

8. What are advancement opportunities? _____

_____

_____

_____

9. What did you think of the working environment? _____

_____

_____

_____

10. In light of this interview, are you encouraged or discouraged about this oc-cupation as a possible career?

_____

_____

_____

_____

Exercise 2

Personality characteristics of person interviewed

1. Can you identify the hero group of the person you interviewed? _____

2. Is your hero the same or different?_____

3. Describe the communication between the two of you with reference to your hero groups.

_____

_____

_____

_____

_____

4. How did this impact your decision about the career?

_____

_____

_____

_____

REMEMBER: The information you are receiving is coming through their hero fil-ter. You will ultimately have to make a decision that is based on your own per-sonality values, skills, and interests.

Chapter 8

Short Journal (5 minutes or less)

What did you learn from this interview?

_____

_____

_____

_____

_____

_____

_____

_____

_____

_____

_____

_____

_____

_____

I have found the best way to give advice to your children is to find out what they want and then advise them to do it.
– Harry S. Truman

FAMILY INFLUENCE ON CAREER DECISIONS

CHAPTER 9

Family Influence on Career Decisions

Take out your Hero Character Cards and rank order them as you did before, but this time rank them for each of your parents. You may ask your parents to rank their own cards. List their primary heroes below:

Father: _____
Mother: _____
Myself: _____

Parents usually set the tone for the family. When a student is not understood by the parents, the cause may be the clash of hero codes and, therefore, a mixture of values. You may be able to relate to this information even if you left home several years ago, and see how your parent's influence, positive or negative, caused you to go in the career direction you have chosen.

On pages that follow, hero combinations illustrate probable family reactions when the same and different parent/child hero combinations are present. But first read about the parenting style of each personality (hero).

THINKER parents will focus on their kids intellectual ability. This will start when the baby is in the crib by buying stimulating toys for them. Instead of saying "goo-goo ga-ga" they will speak in adult language to these infants. They will also begin to read to their babies very early. As soon as their kids can talk they will teach them to speak clearly and in complete sentences. Their children will usually have a large vocabulary very early. Because they don't believe in fostering dependency, they will insist on their kids using their own minds to problem solve and make decisions. They may insist that their child look up an answer in the encyclopedia instead of asking the parents. Children are treated like little adults. Reading and learning are very important to these parents so they will encourage their kids to do the same. Family outings will likely include places like the library and the museum.

HELPER parents are not usually big on discipline. They tend to treat their children in a more democratic way that takes everyone's needs into consideration. Much focus is placed on their kids' emotional well being. It is important to them that their children are happy and feel good about themselves. They like to hug and kiss their kids a lot. They also value self-esteem so highly that they will stress positive things about their kids and sometimes overlook the negative.

Disharmony is so upsetting to them that they strive to keep peace among family members. These parents like to talk to their kids and have them openly express their feelings. If something is bothering the child, a Helper parent will be the first to know. Maintaining a close relationship with their kids is most important to these parents. Often you will see Helper mothers and daughters shopping and doing things together like best girl friends. They encourage their kids to have friends so it is not unusual for them to entertain other kids in their home.

DOER parents probably play this role in the least traditional manner. They are more permissive with their kids and give them more freedom to make decisions. They are also more playful with their kids and sometimes treat them like peers. Other times they will take back their authority role, but they punish less often and with less severity than Planner parents. There tends to be more flexibility in the home in general. Kids may not always go to bed at the same time at night depending on what else is going on in the home, and meals may be served when everyone feels like eating rather than at established times. They like to go out to eat, a decision, like many others, that is often based on how they feel at the moment.

PLANNER parents play their role in the most traditional manner. They establish themselves as the authority figures in the family and demand that children respect them as such. The parents determine the rules that govern the family, and the children are taught to obey these rules or they will be punished. These parents are usually very strict with their kids. Discipline plays a major part in their parenting style and this discipline does not stop at home. They also demand that their children be good citizens who obey the law and other authority figures outside of the home, such as teachers and ministers.

Parental Hero Influences on the Doer Student

Doer Parents
This is a great match! These two share the same values, interests, and energy. Being of the same hero group, they are compatible and easily understand each other. Parent and child of the Doer group will tend to be very active, adventurous, and will seek excitement. Both will compete, enjoy hands-on activities, and be physical and spontaneous. They may encounter some difficulty

arising from competing against each other, or they may create a game of "one-upping" the other.

Planner Parents

This can be a difficult match. It is the classic family clash. These two have very different values and often disagree sharply. The Doer child is a risk-taker desiring action, spontaneity, and adventure. The Planner parent holds traditional values and morals with a definite sense of right and wrong. Treasuring stability, responsibility, and predictability, the Planner parent may have difficulty with the Doer child's impulsiveness, fun-loving spirit, immediate gratification attitude, and drive. The child may also rebel against the rules imposed and their Planner parent's planned, serious approach to life.

Thinker Parents

The Thinker parent and the Doer child share values of getting to the point and in being direct. They are also similar in the drive to compete and to be competent. Difficulties arise when the Thinker parent's futuristic, abstract thinking conflicts with the Doer child's drive for "here and now" action. The controlling nature of the Thinker parent (who has high expectations for perfection and excellence) may be met with rebellion from the Doer child. A big contrast exists with the Doer child who seeks external stimulation and entertainment and the Thinker parent strives to instill internal motivation and quests.

Helper Parents

This combination tends to work, although often at the expense of the Doer child who is learning responsibility. Conflicts can arise due to the Helper parent's talent of empathizing and appreciating uniqueness. At times, the Doer child receives too much flexibility in being himself/herself and does not receive necessary discipline; the child may rebel against the parent's need to communicate and to relate. Doer children are often appreciated and encouraged to be creative and seek possibilities. But the push for honesty and authenticity by the Helper parent may be considered intrusive to the Doer independence. The Helper parent may be seen by the Doer child as a soft-touch, too mellow, and easily manipulated—an art of the Doer child.

Parental Hero Influences on the Planner Student

Doer Parents
The biggest frustration in this combination is the Doer parent's lifestyle of few rules and little structure compared to the Planner child who wants tradition, plans, predictability, and who carries a sense of right and wrong. The playful attitude and spontaneous ventures of the parent is sometimes fun for the child, yet can be embarrassing, as well. Planner children share a need for usefulness of ideas or objects. A cluttered home that the Doer parent allows may be unsightly to the Planner child. The Planner child will tend to worry over the Doer parent's impulsiveness to conquer the unknown.

Planner Parents
This match is brilliant—a golden combination that satisfies and supports both the parents and the child. Both enjoy the clearly defined expectations and the rules established in the household. Things are neat, orderly, and run on a schedule. The consistency and stability of the home is comforting to both parents and child. They mutually support and adhere to tradition and to the laws of home and society. There is a clear sense of the parent being in charge. A great deal of hard work occurs at home and both parents and children excel in work and in school.

Thinker Parents
The Planner child may have difficulty with the futuristic, abstract thinking of the Thinker parent. The child wants more detailed, organized, practical guidance. The Thinker parent's high expectations for competency and perfection will motivate the Planner child to do well, yet may be perceived as too demanding after a reasonable standard has been met.

Helper Parents
This combination shares values of belonging and helping others. Areas of potential difficulty involve the Helper parent's idealistic, searching imagination, which conflicts with the Planner child's need for practical, outlined structure. The Helper parent may be seen as "wishy-washy" and not providing enough "backbone" for family. Often, the Helper parent's searching involves non-traditional activities viewed as ridiculous to the Planner student.

Parental Hero Influences on the Thinker Student

Doer Parents

These two share values of freedom to explore what interests them. They tend to allow room for the other to seek stimulating experiences. The Thinker child thrives on ideas and invention, while the Doer parent quests for adventure on a physical level. The parent may joke about the child being "too stuffy," and the child may joke that the parent is "too wild" or "off the wall." However, they award each other mutual respect, even though the Doer parent may not measure up to the Thinker child's high expectations of perfectionism.

Planner Parents

There are often clashes in this combination. The Planner parent wants to instill in the child values of planning and preparing for a secure future of family, savings, and a dependable, respectable job. The Thinker child tends to value the quest for abstract, futuristic ideas for the sake of invention and the mental challenge. They both tend to have a serious approach to life and avoid physical risks. The Thinker child is very independent and the Planner parent wants to bring him/her into the family unit more than the child desires.

Thinker Parents

Because parent and child share the same values, this is a compatible combination. The Thinker parent and child stimulate and challenge one another's logic, inventions, and wisdom. Both drive for competency and perfection, and feed off each other's projects. They respect each other's need for independence and understand the distance in relationships. Both are powerful people, and there may be some clashes and competition with competency. The child may feel the need to be as good as or better than the parent, and the parent's need to maintain status and control will conflict.

Helper Parents

The Thinker child often feels smothered by the Helper parent. The parent's need for communication, for family cohesion, and for emotional connections is uncomfortable and often viewed as silly by the Thinker child. The Helper parent's feelings of focus and fostering dependency on family is the exact opposite of the Thinker child's quest for knowledge and independence.

Parental Hero Influences on the Helper Student

Doer Parents

The Helper child has an understanding of the parent's need for adventure and impulsive actions. The child enjoys the parent's fun-loving sense of humor, but is easily hurt by the parent's to-the-point directness. Parent and child share the quest for possibilities, yet the parent is the greater risk-taker of the two. The Helper child is not competitive like the parent, but rather seeks cohesion, harmony, and a "working together" relationship. The Helper child can seem too needy to the on-the-go Doer parent. The Helper child may feel neglected and a lack of being nurtured.

Planner Parents

The Helper child complies with the Planner parent's rules and structure at home, yet may behave differently with friends in order to fit in. Parent and child share the need to belong and the dependency on family. They separate as the Helper child grows older and relies more on friends. The Helper child strives for harmony and may not be direct with the truth with the Planner parent who expects adherence to right and wrong, according to the rules of the family. The Helper child's idealism and the realism of the Planner parent can at times clash.

Thinker Parents

This combination often leaves the Helper child starved for attention due to the Thinker parent's preoccupation with ideas and abstractions. The parent's need for independence and distance from frequent emotional connections or demonstrations overshadows the Helper Child's striving for affection, relating, and communicating. The child's value of sensitivity and empathy of feelings is in opposition to the parent's value of logic and knowledge. The Helper child may feel the Thinker parent is too harsh and demanding in expecting competency and perfection. The child may strive to meet these expectations to please and may never feel quite good enough.

Helper Parents

This is a satisfying combination for both parent and child. The compatibility of their values meets needs for relationships, communication, sensitivity, and understanding. This combination can also result in an extremely dependent parent/child relationship to the detriment of both. The child may put so much energy into taking care of and pleasing the parent that he/she becomes stunted in terms of mental development.

Exercise 1

Relationship with your mother

Which combination describes your relationship with your mother?

_____

_____

What insights have you gained from the description?

_____

_____

_____

_____

Compare your values with those of your mother. Discuss how they are compatible or how they clash.

_____

_____

_____

_____

_____

How does your mother feel about your career choices?

_____

_____

_____

_____

_____

_____

_____

What impact has this had on you?

_____

_____

_____

_____

_____

_____

_____

Exercise 2

Relationship with your father

Which combination describes your relationship with your father?

_____

_____

What insights have you gained from the description?

_____

_____

_____

_____

Compare your values with those of your father. Discuss how they are compat-ible or how they clash.

_____

_____

_____

_____

_____

How does you father feel about your career choices?

_____

_____

_____

_____

_____

What impact has this had on you?

_____

_____

_____

_____

_____

_____

When you understand that people see the world through their own filters, you will see why your parents may view the world differently than you. Therefore, you will also see why the career choices they might want for you may be different from the choices you make for yourself.

Chapter 9

Short Journal (5 minutes or less)

What I have learned about myself in this chapter is

_____

_____

_____

_____

_____

_____

_____

_____

_____

_____

_____

_____

_____

_____

A teacher affects eternity; he can
never tell where his influence stops
– Henry Brooks Adams

TEACHER'S INFLUENCE

Chapter 10

Teacher's Influence

Teaching Styles

Teaching styles differ depending on the teacher's hero or personality. Personal values dictate what motivates a person's behavior and therefore indicates what your teachers will focus their attention on in the classroom. The lists below show the values of each hero teacher.

The Doer Teacher Values:

Spontaneity
Creativity
The unusual and out-of-the-ordinary
Hands-on activities
Concrete materials
Immediate results
Short-term goals
Energy, vitality, movement
Physical activity
Cleverness
Attention
Skills

The Planner Teacher Values:

Student achievement and performance
Proper student behavior
Lack of classroom disruptions
Student punctuality
Classroom rules established and obeyed
Organization and structure
Tradition (the tried and true)
Lecture method of delivering instruction
Subject-oriented classroom activities
Exactness
Hard work
Long-term goals

The Thinker Teacher Values:
Freedom
Independent thought
Mental activity
Individuality
Ingenuity
Self-control
Competence
Subject- or knowledge-oriented classroom activities
Independent study and projects
Problem-solving approach to instruction
Inquiry and discovery methods of instruction
Future outcomes

The Helper Teacher Values:
Being able to relate to students on a personal level
Giving help to students (academic and social)
A "good feeling tone" in his/her classroom
The esteem of all those in his/her class
Harmony
Understanding
People-oriented concepts and activities
Influencing others for their "good"
Cooperative learning
Imagination and creativity
Success for everyone

Personal Motivation Determines Learning Styles . . . and Which Teachers are Compatible

The purpose of this chapter is to reveal your ideal teacher, discuss your ideal learning environment, and help you understand what motivates you to learn. Because we don't all learn the same way, it is important to know what motivates you. This knowledge will help you understand why you learn from some teachers and not from others.

Respond to the following according to your first hero.

DOER STUDENTS
Learning Motivators
- Perform well in competition, especially when there is a lot of action
- Love games and "hands-on" activities
- Love fun and excitement
- Have difficulty with routine or structured presentations
- Receive a kick out of putting what they have learned to immediate use
- Perform best when they can apply skills learned in school to the world
- in which they live
- Learn by doing

Atmosphere in which Doer Students Learn Best
- Spontaneous
- Animated, active
- Humorous
- Interactive
- Minimal lectures
- Friendly

Exercise 1

Positive learning experience

Give an example of a positive learning experience that you have had.

_____

_____

_____

_____

_____

_____

_____

_____

_____

_____

_____

_____

What is the relationship between this experience and what motivates you to learn?

_____

_____

_____

_____

_____

_____

_____

_____

_____

Looking at Teachers from the Doer Perspective

Doer Teacher: A good match with the Doer student. The student is likely to maintain the greatest rapport with an Doer teacher. The student appreciates the atmosphere of freedom and spontaneity in this teacher's classroom and responds favorably to the "hands-on" approach to learning. Both teacher and student enjoy games and competition and are tireless in their efforts to complete any job at hand.

Exercise 2

Experience with an Doer teacher

Describe an experience that you had with this type of teacher.

_____

_____

_____

_____

_____

_____

_____

_____

_____

_____

Looking at Teachers from the Doer Perspective

Planner Teacher: The Planner teacher's demands for order, organization, and appropriate behavior in the classroom do not conform well with the Doer student's need for spontaneity, fun, and quick action. The Planner teacher emphasizes rules and facts, as well as neatness and structure. The Doer student may react with various degrees of rebellion and hostility when confronted with a Planner classroom atmosphere.

Exercise 3

Experience with a Planner teacher

Describe an experience you had with this type of teacher.

_____

_____

_____

_____

_____

_____

_____

_____

_____

Looking at Teachers from the Doer Perspective

Thinker Teacher: The Thinker teacher is often capable of creating an atmosphere of independence, freedom of thought, and action in his classroom. This climate allows the Doer student to express his needs.

Exercise 4

Experience with a Thinker teacher

Describe an experience that you had with this type of teacher.

_____

_____

_____

_____

_____

_____

_____

_____

_____

_____

Looking at Teachers from the Doer Perspective

Helper Teacher: The Helper teacher can have some empathy for the Doer student's needs, and this teacher's good sense of humor is protection from reacting too harshly to the Doer student's demands for fun and entertainment. The Doer student may require more "hands-on" activities, games, and competition than are normally scheduled in the lesson plans of the Helper teacher.

Exercise 5

Experience with a Helper teacher

Describe an experience that you had with this type of teacher.

_____

_____

_____

_____

_____

_____

_____

_____

_____

PLANNER STUDENTS
Learning Motivators
- Do their best when the course content is structured and clearly defined
- Want to know when they are on the right track
- Are greatly helped by rules and directions
- Thrive on routine and orderliness

Atmosphere in which Planner Students Learn Best
- Structured
- Tasks clearly stated
- Organized
- Clear expectations

Exercise 1

Positive learning experiences

Give an example of a positive learning experience that you have had.

_____

_____

_____

_____

What is the relationship between this experience and what motivates you to learn?

_____

_____

_____

_____

Looking at Teachers from the Planner Perspective

Doer Teacher: This combination can be somewhat problematic. The Planner student prefers organized, structured, and predictable routines, while the Doer teacher tends to prefer an atmosphere of spontaneity and excitement. The Planner student may often complain that tasks are never completed and that he does not learn much of anything in the Doer teacher's classroom. The Planner student strives for perfection and enjoys being validated for neat and accurate work.

Exercise 2

Experience with an Doer teacher

Describe an experience that you had with this type of teacher.

_____

_____

_____

_____

_____

_____

_____

_____

_____

Looking at Teachers from the Planner Perspective

Planner Teacher: This is a suitable match. The Planner student is likely to maintain the greatest rapport and cooperation with the Planner teacher. The student appreciates the structure, organization, and rules that the Planner teacher emphasizes. The Planner student responds well to this teacher's style of presenting material which is based on logical procedures and clearly defined factual information.

Exercise 3

Experience with a Planner teacher

Describe an experience that you had with this type of teacher.

_____

_____

_____

_____

_____

_____

_____

_____

_____

Looking at Teachers from the Planner Perspective

Thinker Teacher: The Thinker teacher may not always meet the needs of the Planner student for clear and concise rules and regulations. The independent thinking, originality, and mental creativity so valued by this Thinker teacher will not be highly appreciated by the Planner student. The Planner student may experience anxiety and difficulty related to grasping conceptual matter if it is not explained and demonstrated in concrete ways.

Exercise 4

Experience with a Thinker teacher

Describe an experience that you had with this type of teacher.

_____

_____

_____

_____

_____

_____

_____

_____

_____

Looking at Teachers from the Planner Perspective

Helper Teacher: The Planner student responds well to the Helper teacher's classroom atmosphere if a regular and predictable schedule is maintained. The Planner student requires rules and facts, as well as organized, accurate, and logical procedures. The Helper teacher and the Planner student may differ in expression of response to very deep emotions. Although the Planner student follows rules and accomplishes well-structures work, the creativity valued by the Helper teacher may rarely be exhibited.

Exercise 5

Experience with a Helper teacher

Describe an experience that you had with this type of teacher.

_____

_____

_____

_____

_____

_____

_____

_____

_____

THINKER STUDENTS
Learning Motivators
- Perform best when exposed to the driving force or overall theory behind a subject
- Prefer to work independently
- Aroused by new ideas and concepts, and enjoy interpreting them before adding them to their bank of knowledge
- Need to be challenged
- Like to be recognized and appreciated for their competence in a subject

Atmosphere in which Thinker Students Learn Best
- Academically demanding
- Encouragement to learn more
- Energetic programs

Exercise 1

Positive learning experiences

Give an example of a positive learning experience that you have had.

_____

_____

_____

_____

What is the relationship between this experience and what motivates you to learn?

_____

_____

_____

_____

Looking at Teachers from the Thinker Perspective

Doer Teacher: The Thinker student responds well to the classroom atmosphere of the Doer teacher if attracted to the subject matter, and if allowed to express and discuss personal ideas. The Thinker student is creative and enjoys discovering new ways of solving problems. Unlike the Doer teacher, the Thinker student values ideas and concepts above immediate action and wants to inquire about the principles behind each task.

Exercise 2

Experience with an Doer teacher

Describe an experience that you had with this type of teacher.

_____

_____

_____

_____

_____

_____

_____

_____

_____

Looking at Teachers from the Thinker Perspective

Planner Teacher: This combination works only if the Thinker student is sufficiently interested in the subject matter and given some freedom to explore ideas and concepts beyond the requirements of the class. Unlike the Planner teacher, the Thinker student can be oblivious to rules and regulations. It will be difficult to gain the Thinker student's cooperation without a perception that rules are logical and necessary.

Exercise 3

Experience with a Planner teacher

Describe an experience that you had with this type of teacher.

_____

_____

_____

_____

_____

_____

_____

_____

_____

Looking at Teachers from the Thinker Perspective

Thinker Teacher: The Thinker student will likely maintain the greatest rapport and cooperation with Thinker teachers. The student appreciates the stimulating and creative environment provided by the Thinker teacher and enjoys discussing ideas, investigating relationships between principles, and discovering new ways of solving problems—especially in conjunction with the Thinker teacher.

Exercise 4

Experience with a Thinker teacher

Describe an experience that you had with this type of teacher.

_____

_____

_____

_____

_____

_____

_____

_____

_____

Looking at Teachers from the Thinker Perspective

Helper Teacher: The Thinker student responds well to the classroom atmosphere of the Helper teacher, as long as the student's interest in the subject matter and curiosity is continually reinforced. Unlike the Helper teacher, the Thinker student is less concerned with the feelings of others and will tend to express opinions regardless of how they may affect the feelings of others.

Exercise 5

Experience with a Helper teacher

Describe an experience that you had with this type of teacher.

_____

_____

_____

_____

_____

_____

_____

_____

_____

HELPER STUDENTS
Learning Motivators
- Feel best in an open, interactive atmosphere
- Like to feel that their teachers really care about them, and that they give the class a personal touch
- Appreciate supportive attention and feedback
- Thrive in a "humanistic," people-oriented environment
- "Turn-off" when conflicts arise, and flourish in an atmosphere of cooperation
- Important that teachers value and respect their feelings

Atmosphere in which Helper Students Learn Best
- Warm
- Relaxed
- Creative
- Flexible
- Personal
- Caring, happy
- Discussion-oriented
- Freedom to experiment

Exercise 1

Positive learning experiences

Give an example of a positive learning experience that you have had.

_____

_____

_____

_____

_____

_____

What is the relationship between this experience and what motivates you to learn?

_____

_____

_____

_____

Looking at Teachers from the Helper Perspective

Doer Teacher: This combination can work well if the Doer teacher allows the Helper student to be creative and show personal concern. The Helper student appreciates the good sense of humor of the Doer teacher. The student may have difficulty making quick decisions and could become bogged down before completing a task. Although the Helper student values communication and social interaction, the Doer teacher's direct mode of criticism and comments may not be appreciated.

Exercise 2

Experience with an Doer teacher

Describe an experience that you had with this type of teacher.

_____

_____

_____

_____

Looking at Teachers from the Helper Perspective

Planner Teacher: The Helper student adheres to the rules of the Planner teacher as long as they seem fair and there is personal consideration and compassion given to the student. The Helper student will cooperate, particularly if it is felt the Planner teacher likes and cares for the individuality of the student. Unlike the Planner teacher, the Helper student tends to be emotional and allow feelings to interfere with academic work. This student's need to socialize may also be viewed as highly disruptive by the Planner teacher.

Exercise 3

Experience with a Planner teacher

Describe an experience that you had with this type of teacher.

_____

_____

_____

_____

_____

_____

_____

_____

_____

Looking at Teachers from the Helper Perspective

Thinker Teacher: The Helper student responds well to the classroom atmosphere of the Thinker teacher, as long as it is personally relevant and stimulating to a creative imagination. The Helper student is motivated to perform in an effort to please the teacher, rather than to demonstrate intellectual mastery of a concept. Unlike the Thinker teacher, this student tends to value feelings and interpersonal communication above ideas and concepts. Some potential for friction exists due to this difference in values.

Exercise 4

Experience with a Thinker teacher

Describe an experience that you had with this type of teacher.

_____

_____

_____

_____

_____

_____

_____

_____

Looking at Teachers from the Helper Perspective

Helper Teacher: The Helper student will likely maintain the greatest rapport and cooperation with the Helper teacher. The Helper student appreciates the fairness, sensitivity, and personal concern expressed by the Helper teacher. The atmosphere of imaginative creativity and social interaction provided by the Helper teacher is highly appealing to the Helper student.

Exercise 5

Experience with a Helper teacher

Describe an experience that you had with this type of teacher.

_____

_____

_____

_____

_____

_____

_____

_____

_____

_____

Exercise 6

Determining The Inner Heroes of My Teachers

List your current instructors and their Inner Heroes. If you cannot determine their hero groups, ask them to rank the cards themselves.

1. _____

2. _____

3. _____

4. _____

5. _____

Now, discuss your learning experiences with each instructor.
1. _____

_____

_____

_____

2. _____

_____

_____

_____

3. _____

_____

_____

_____

4. _____

_____

_____

_____

5. _____

_____

_____

_____

You may not always have your ideal teacher for every class. But by under-standing what motivates you to learn and the atmosphere in which you learn best, you will be able to take more responsibility for your own experience.

Exercise 7

Multiple Intelligence

There are many ways besides IQ (intelligence quotient) to measure intellect. Dr. Howard Gardner, a psychologist, has identified seven kinds of intelligence which he calls multiple intelligences. Another psychologist, Dr. Thomas Armstrong says there are seven kinds of smarts. These different ways in which people are talented are listed below.

Circle all the ways you think you are smart or intelligent.

1. Musical Intelligence   Music smart

2. Bodily–Kinesthetic Intelligence   Body smart

3. Interpersonal Intelligence   People smart

4. Intrapersonal Intelligence   Self-smart

5. Visual–Spatial Intelligence   Picture smart

6. Linguistic Intelligence   Word smart

7. Logical–Mathematical Intelligence   Logic smart

8. Naturalistic   Nature smart

Dr. Daniel Goleman says we also have an EQ (emotional quotient)—your ability to handle your emotions. He believes it is the most important form of intelligence because it determines how happy and successful you will be.

Exercise 8

Inner Heroes & Intelligence

Your inner Heroes are another method of understanding how you are smart. Each Hero is intelligent in a different way. Your first Hero represents your major strengths and your unique kind of smartness. Below discuss your special talents and how that relates to your career choice. (Your Hero cards can be helpful.)

Helper Intelligence

_____

_____

Thinker Intelligence

_____

_____

_____

Planner Intelligence

_____

_____

_____

Doer Intelligence

_____

_____

_____

Exercise 9

The Need to Manage Your Weaknesses

The most well rounded people have developed several parts of their personality—areas that need to be managed in order to be successful. Consider which of the areas above you need to strengthen so that you are more well rounded in things such as work, finances, and relationships. Since your last hero represents your most challenging areas, use the space below to discuss what you need to do to improve in that area.

Example: My last Hero is Planner. I need to work on balancing my check-book and organizing my desk.

My last Hero is _____.

What I need to do to strengthen this area in my life is _____

_____

_____

_____

_____

Chapter 10

Short Journal (5 minutes of less)

What new insights do you have about the way you learn best?

_____

_____

_____

_____

_____

_____

_____

_____

_____

_____

_____

_____

_____

_____

_____

_____

_____

_____

_____

_____

_____

_____

_____

_____

The tragedy of life doesn't lie in reaching your goal. The tragedy lies in having no goal to reach.
– Benjamin E. Mays

Chapter 11

DECISION-MAKING & GOAL-SETTING

Chapter 11

Decision-Making and Goal-Setting

Goals are the things that you want to accomplish because they have meaning to you. They should be realistic enough for you to believe they are possible, but at the same time not compromise your dreams. Some goals are short-term while others are long-term. A short-term goal might be to get a good grade in your higher math class so that you can accomplish a long-term goal of being accepted into a university.

Now that you have gained more knowledge about yourself and what you desire in your life, it is time to make it happen. Only you can take responsibility for your own life and accomplish your goals. It is important to keep a positive mental attitude that says "yes, I can." If you believe you can—you can! Of course, the opposite is also true. If you believe you can't—you are also right. It's your choice.

Exercise 1

Most desirable career

Take the most desirable choice from your list of 5 top careers in chapter 7, and complete the following exercise which includes some of your short-term goals.

Career Choice _____

This career is my first choice because _____

_____

_____

_____

_____

Hitch your wagon to a star.
- Ralph Waldo Emerson

What I need to do within 6 months to accomplish my goal is _____

_____

_____

_____

_____

_____

What I need to do within 1 year to accomplish my goal is _____

_____

_____

_____

_____

_____

The barriers I need to overcome to reach my goal are _____

_____

_____

_____

_____

I plan to achieve my goal by _____(date).

Exercise 2

Personal goals

While making decisions about the direction you want to take in your life don't forget to include personal goals. Balance in your personal and professional life is very important. You are not just a human being that has physical needs. You also have mental, emotional and spiritual needs. Make a list of your goals that address more of your personal needs.

Example: I will exercise 3 times a week, or I will listen to a motivational tape everyday for inspiration.

1. _____

2. _____

3. _____

4. _____

5. _____

6. _____

7. _____

Exercise 3

Long-term goals

It is also important to set long-term goals—those that take more time to accomplish. The more goals you can set for your life the more direction you will have.

Can you think of other goals you would like to accomplish in:

5 years

1. _____

2. _____

3. _____

4. _____

5. _____

10 years

1. _____

2. _____

3. _____

4. _____

5. _____

20 years

1. _____

2. _____

3. _____

4. _____

5. _____

Exercise 4

My legacy

What Legacy do You Want to Leave?

One way to set goals is to look backwards. What contribution would you like to make that continues to benefit others long after your lifetime? Use the space below to write your legacy. It may generate more goals to add to your list.

_____

_____

_____

_____

_____

_____

_____

_____

_____

_____

_____

_____

_____

_____

_____

_____

_____

_____

_____

_____

_____

_____

_____

_____

The Need for Lifelong Learning

Old paradigms in the workplace don't apply anymore. The future trend is for workers to have several temporary jobs rather than one permanent one. This puts you in a position of always seeking new opportunities for which you need to have a competitive edge.

You must be responsible for your continuous learning and keeping your skills up-to-date. Companies are no longer sharing in this responsibility. They expect you to do whatever is necessary on your own time. Be prepared to take courses and workshops, read books and journals, and develop new skills.

Exercise 5

Lifelong learning goals

The best time to prepare for lifelong learning is now. Think about and list below some other ideas for your continuous growth.

Example: additional degrees, start a foundation, learn to write a book.

_____

_____

_____

_____

_____

_____

_____

_____

_____

_____

_____

Recommendations

1. Read Carolyn Kalil's book **Follow Your Inner Heroes™ to the Work You Love** for a better understanding of yourself and your ideal career.

2. Develop a resume. The purpose of your resume is to let potential employers know that you are interested in interviewing for an available job opportunity. Visit a career center to learn about necessary content and format options. Electronic resumes are becoming quite popular.

3. Learn interviewing techniques. See a career counselor to improve your interviewing skills.

4. Contact www.innerheroes.com and www.carolynkalil.com for information about other products and training.